BORDERTOWN CLASHES, RESOURCE WARS, AND CONTESTED TERRITORIES

THE FOUR CORNERS IN THE TURBULENT 1970S

BORDERTOWN CLASHES, RESOURCE WARS, AND CONTESTED TERRITORIES

THE FOUR CORNERS IN THE TURBULENT 1970S

John Redhouse

Brooklyn, NY
Philadelphia, PA
commonnotions.org

ISBN: 978-1-945335-27-3 | eBook ISBN: 978-1-945335-57-0
Library of Congress Number: 2025936101
10 9 8 7 6 5 4 3 2 1

Common Notions   Common Notions
c/o Interference Archive   c/o Making Worlds Bookstore
314 7th St.   210 S. 45th St.
Brooklyn, NY 11215   Philadelphia, PA 19104

www.commonnotions.org
info@commonnotions.org

Published with Red Media Press
editor@redmedia.press
redmedia.press

Discounted bulk quantities of our books are available for organizing, educational, or fundraising purposes. Please contact Common Notions at the
address above for more information.

Cover design by Josh MacPhee
Layout design and typesetting by Sydney Rainer
Printed by union labor in Canada on acid-free paper

CONTENTS

FOREWORD

Jennifer Denetdale

I am a historian—the first Diné to earn a PhD in history. I was taught to read the English language when I was five years old, taking my parents' message that education was important to heart. My parents were boarding school survivors who met at Stewart Indian School in Stewart, Nevada and equated "education" with an American education. After their boarding school experience, they decided not to expect their five children to speak our own language, Diné bizaad, even though they spoke our language to each other and within our Diné community every day of their lives. They must have experienced shame for being Diné and speaking our language. So, like many Diné and Indigenous children, I experienced the ethnic cleansing policies of the American settler state first-hand. Thus, my first language was English, Biláaganaa bizaad. When I get lonely for my parents, I listen to our people speak and sing our language. It is a form of resistance. As far back as I remember, I understood our language.

Much of my childhood was spent in an El Paso Natural Gas Company employee housing compound on Navajo Nation land near Ganado, then Tohatchi, and later Montezuma Creek. I observed and felt what I later learned to identify as racism and discrimination, but I didn't have a language for it. It wasn't until I started reading and studying Indigenous writers that I could name what I observed and felt. My father's boarding school education also fostered his respect for books, so there were always books in our home.

Indian education was not assimilation, as apologists prefer to call it. It was genocidal and a form of ethnic cleansing. We were supposed to disappear into the ravages of the US capitalistic system and then die slowly. We were to forget that we are the descendants of the original peoples of this land and that we lived in freedom. Our Diné had once created powerful alliances with other Indigenous peoples in what is now called the American Southwest. Our language was the language our allies learned to be in relations with us.

The Spaniards invaded our territory, searched for wealth, and enslaved our women and children. Our name for ourselves—"Navajo" or "Naabeehó"—was corrupted by these invaders and settlers. The Naakai (Spaniards and Mexicans) and the Pueblo people—our once allies turned enemies—claimed the word meant "thief" or interchangeably "planters of fields." On a hot summer morning under a tent in Tohatchi, one of our revered elders told us that the word "Naabeehó" meant "Naabaahíí" or "warriors." We are warrior people and when we met other peoples, we told them our name was "Naabaahíí," warrior people.

Cut to Red Power Rising, when the Indigenous people of this land rose and faced down the relentless violence of colonizers, including the settler state's claims of ownership over our land and lives. The histories foreigners wrote of themselves were one of the tools used to continually legitimize their violence against our people. I was in my teens when Red Power rose and took shape around me. I looked on with curiosity as I observed young Diné protesting with signs outside the annual Gallup Ceremonial—against the hawking of our culture for tourists who wanted to see dancing Indians. At twelve or thirteen years old, I didn't understand the growing Indigenous and Diné rebellion against American colonial rule, but I knew what Indian hating was. Anti-Indianism is woven into the fabric of American society. It is the structure of our dispossession and still has life. In those years of on-the-ground resistance,

I was undoubtedly in the same spaces as John Redhouse. I lived in Tohatchi when Larry Casuse stood his ground and sacrificed his life on March 1, 1973, murdered by the City of Gallup.

In the nineties, I came across the John Redhouse Collection in the Southwest Research Center at the University of New Mexico. In a column in the *Navajo Times,* he castigated our leaders for agreeing to extinguish our land claims, a process that began in the US Indian Land Claims Commission. Our Navajo Nation land was nickel and dimed. Extinguishing our claims to aboriginal land was yet another way the federal government effectively absolved itself of any responsibility for its crimes against Indigenous people and continues to do so.

John's vision that our Indigenous people had the right to live in freedom and independence still resonates with me. In him, I found a relative who told me the truth about Diné dispossession. I discovered that his words matched his actions. In the seventies, John was a mover and shaker who stood on the line of resistance and never wavered.

Our Diné tradition of resistance has foundations in our repertoire of ceremonies, prayers, and songs. They are our history of our creation, how we came to regard the universe, earth and sky, the sun, as our caretakers and our protectors. Every time we relay our Blessings and acknowledge our Holy People, *Diyiin Diné,* we recreate ourselves as freedom-loving Diné, Naabaahíí.

Our resistance takes many forms and one of those is reflected in the life's work of John Redhouse. He is the Naabaahíí that our stories speak of—a warrior. His stories in this volume cast light on a formative period of Diné life under American colonialism. In our stories, including those like John's, we see ourselves in our best light, as a people who have always stood on the frontlines against the violence of the settlers and their settler state. Our light does not diminish, as John shows us. Our spirit of resistance as Diné and Indigenous shines in John's story—a story that we should tell our young people and use to remind our elders of our warrior spirit.

INTRODUCTION

Melanie K. Yazzie

NEVER BACK DOWN

September 21, 2024, was an unusually hot day. The weather forecast predicted the temperature would peak at seventy degrees Fahrenheit around four o'clock in the afternoon. However, the sun already commanded the cloudless sky with blinding light and intense heat as people began filling an empty parking lot at the intersection of Broadway and Main in Farmington, New Mexico around nine o'clock in the morning. Over the next hour, people filtered in wearing ribbon and saanii skirts, carrying American Indian Movement (AIM) flags, clutching bottles of water, and holding signs and banners. Around ten o'clock, the crowd proceeded to the south entrance of the parking lot to begin marching east on Broadway, eventually stopping at the historic Totah Theater on Main Street, where a two-hour-long event was held immediately following the march. Those in attendance had gathered to commemorate a historic uprising in 1974, fifty years prior, following the brutal torture and murder of three Diné men by three white teenagers in Farmington. The Chokecherry Massacre murders sparked outrage from our people, who were fed up with discrimination, racism, and violence against their relatives in reservation bordertowns like Farmington. They organized one of the largest and longest-running protests in Diné history, drawing thousands of Native people from across Turtle Island to march on Farmington for weeks on end.[1]

While many of the heroes of 1974 had since passed on in their journey, several key leaders from the uprising spoke at the commemoration event. Now elders, they recounted the events of that "long hot summer" of mobilization. Chili Yazzie, one of the commemoration's organizers and a key participant in the 1974 uprising, opened the event. He relayed an oral history of the resistance, recalling the moment when AIM came from South Dakota at the behest of Larry Anderson, another Diné leader in the uprising. Yazzie used the term *doo nídaaldzid da*—they were not afraid—to describe AIM. He also recalled how, in the aftermath of the brutal killings, the Diné people *doo nídalyééś da*—acted without hesitation. By all accounts, they enacted justice and demonstrated great courage by staring down the enemy or, as Jennifer Nez Denetdale writes, "rose up in revolt against hundreds of years of settler violence," unafraid "to stand up for Indigenous freedom."[2]

About an hour later, John Redhouse rose from his seat to deliver a speech. Among his many contributions to Diné liberation (detailed in this memoir), Redhouse was a leader of great courage in the 1974 uprising. He approached the podium to thunderous applause; it was a reception for a warrior, a hero of the people, someone who acts with neither fear nor hesitation. Known for his powerful and stirring oratory, Redhouse spoke for over forty minutes about that summer, moving seamlessly between the events and actors on the

---

1 The first march on May 4, 1974 drew approximately 4,000 people and subsequent marches—held weekly for four consecutive weeks from May 11 to June 1—drew several thousand (2,000 to 3,000) each. As Redhouse notes, the following week, on June 8, the Main Street Riot was followed by mass arrests and a state injunction that was successfully challenged in federal district court about one month later. After that, the marches resumed until late August, when the New Mexico State Advisory Committee to the US Civil Rights Commission held three days of public hearings in Farmington. Redhouse details this history in Chapter 2.

2 Email correspondence, September 30, 2024.

ground and the larger historical and structural context of settler aggression in the region. As readers will find in *Bordertown Clashes*, Redhouse's sharp mind for historical detail is matched only by his exacting analysis of power. He uses precise language and concise prose. In fact, he writes like he speaks. He holds nothing back when condemning the depredation and harm of resource extraction and bordertown violence. One can only walk away from these pages with a fire for justice lit in their soul. This is the extraordinary quality of an intellectual who is also a warrior. Such people stop you in your tracks—they wield words like arrows to weaken the enemy while simultaneously lifting the hearts of their people, giving them courage and strength to, as Redhouse stated, "never back down."[3]

In her foreword to this memoir, Denetdale reminds us that the Diné are a "freedom-loving people." Both historically and today, our warriors remind us of this fact. She notes that we traditionally introduced ourselves to outsiders as *naabaahíí*, or "warrior people." While warriors are sometimes called activists, I believe this is a misnomer. To walk without fear or hesitation, to never back down, to exhibit courage and encouragement, and to hold always an unwavering love for one's people and land, is the path of a warrior. This is their unique gift; they embody liberation with every breath and beat of their heart. With each word they speak or write, they remind us of who we are and what it is to be free. They give us the courage to be defiantly ourselves.

Warrior intellectuals do not need institutional approval to carry Diné intellectual traditions forward. John Redhouse's prolific output and superb work demonstrate this more clearly than perhaps any other figure in twentieth or twenty-first-century Diné intellectual history. I am a Diné intellectual positioned within academic institutions, but Redhouse never took that path. He has maintained his independence and freedom. He is a true people's historian, a peo-

---

3 John Redhouse, *Remarks at the Fiftieth Year Commemoration of the 1974 Protest and Boycott of Farmington, New Mexico*, at the Totah Theater, Farmington, New Mexico, September 21, 2024.

ple's intellectual. Intellectuals, like warriors and everyone else, are forged from their social and political conditions. They do not belong to a special, elite class that exists above and apart from the people (despite some in the intellectual class who wield their authority to gatekeep).

I would argue that many of our great leaders over time have been warrior intellectuals. Yet we misrecognize them as "activists," deride them as "burn down the fort" Indians, or worse, refuse to take them seriously as intellectuals. Redhouse's life's work defies these categories. In fact, he offers an unparalleled model of what it means to be a Diné intellectual, warrior or otherwise. This memoir proves why we need *more* Diné people to follow in Redhouse's footsteps.

ON COWARDS AND WARRIORS

The Chokecherry Massacre was named after the Chokecherry Canyon, where the bodies of three Diné men were found in 1974. The canyon, a secluded location just north of town, is known to be a favorite site for white residents of Farmington to "roll" Diné people. Rolling includes harassment, humiliation, verbal degradation, kidnapping, physical assault, rape, torture, immolation, and murder. Indian rollers hunt for vulnerable Diné people in town, targeting those out late at night, sleeping on the street, or who are mentally or physically impaired. They lure their targets into vehicles and drive them to places like Chokecherry Canyon to brutalize them, typically leaving them injured or dead in these isolated locations on the outskirts of town.

Indian rolling is a particular kind of blood sport unique to white supremacy in reservation bordertowns. It upholds the age-old tradition of anti-Indianism at the heart of the American project, which secured its national identity through the dispossession of Native land and the genocide of Native people. Historically, Indian rollers worked in packs—settler militias who hunted Native people for scalp bounties. They coexisted with the larger profession of Indian killing—the specialty of the US Cavalry and, later, the police. Like their state-sanctioned counterparts, militias were the foot soldiers of the settler order working on behalf of the US state as it sought to expand westward. They would clear the land for white settlement by eliminating Native people and destroying Native claims to the land that could challenge US possession and obstruct national growth.

While some Indian killers likely saw it as their duty to vanquish a perceived enemy of American civilization, archived photographs of scalp bounties and military correspondence also reveal a sadistic hatred for Native people. This sadistic hatred motivated the kinds of contemporary Indian rolling that occurred in 1974. The grotesquely gratuitous nature of the Chokecherry killings—which I will not detail to honor the dignity of those slain—was so extreme that one has to imagine an element of pleasure infused in the hatred those white teenagers held for our people, a hatred they carved into the bodies of three of our men.

Settler bloodlust in bordertowns is not much different today. The bodies of two Diné men were discovered in an empty lot on the west side of Albuquerque, New Mexico in late July 2014. They had been bludgeoned beyond recognition. A third person, also Diné, was also targeted but narrowly escaped with their life. The attackers were soon identified as three Hispanic teenagers, not unlike those who committed the Chokecherry Massacre forty years prior. They confessed to killing the Diné men as they slept, unable to defend themselves. As Laura Gómez argues, Hispanos in New Mexico serve as a buffer race between Natives and whites.[4] Their position in white supremacy's racial hierarchy shifts based on historical and material conditions and proximity to Indigeneity and whiteness (the pinnacle). White supremacy classifies Hispanos along this racial scale to maintain racial hierarchy under changing conditions. Hispanos, therefore, sometimes serve the interests of white supremacy by upholding settler order in bordertown spaces, granting them proximity to whiteness and power.

---

4 Laura Gómez, *Manifest Destinies: The Making of the Mexican American Race* (New York: NYU Press, 2007).

In both instances of Indian rolling, young white and Hispano men occupy the subject position of settler. Indian rollers represent and reproduce settler order through the ultimate act of anti-Indianism: Indian killing. I imagine Indian killers see themselves as warriors of a certain kind, whether unconsciously or intentionally. The blood sport of bounty hunting, especially when the target is considered an enemy of America, must be thrilling for them, granting them a sense of purpose and glory while fortifying their masculinity. This is the typical image of a warrior ingrained in the American psyche through film and television, video games, and advertisements for military enlistment. Similarly, contemporary US counterinsurgency strategists interpolate the figure of Geronimo, the revered nineteenth-century Apache medicine man and warrior, into modern-day "terrorists" like Osama bin Laden.

Yet, I submit that a different term applies to Indian killers: cowards. Only a coward would target the most vulnerable of our relatives like the unsheltered, the elderly, hitchhikers, teenage girls running alone on dusty reservation roads, women engaged in the sex trade, or those impaired by drugs and alcohol. Cowardice is murdering hundreds of unarmed women, elders, and children at Wounded Knee; abducting and mutilating dozens of First Nations women in Vancouver, British Columbia; and murdering those sleeping out in the open on the streets of reservation bordertowns. Cowardice mingles with greed and anti-Indianism to manifest the heinous reality of Murdered and Missing Indigenous Women and Relatives (MMIWR). MMIWR is the settler order, replete with its bloodlust for dead Indians.

The story is quite different when Indian killers have had to confront our warriors, those members of our nations who belong to a powerful intergenerational association of protectors whose fierceness against the enemy is matched only by their love for the people. Native warriors from various Indigenous nations regularly defeated the US Army until the mid-nineteenth century. Diné warriors were among these heroes. Throughout the eighteenth and nineteenth centuries, Diné warriors resisted Spanish, Mexican, and American encroachment into Diné land. Thomas Dodge, a former chairman of the Navajo tribal council and son of important Diné headman Chee Dodge, wrote of this period:

> Navajos in scattered groups and armed with only primitive weapons of bows and arrows tried to ward off the ever-increasing aggression of the white man by going on frequent raids into the growing settlements along the Rio Grande River in New Mexico. At first these forays were purely defensive measures to keep the white man from grabbing the most desirable of the Indian country. Then the raids became fierce actions of revenge and reprisal against the Spaniard and his Pueblo allies whose raiding parties began to capture and carry off Navajo women and children after slaying the men without any merciful discrimination.[5]

It is true that some Diné began engaging in more gratuitous warfare against settlers. However, we must not forget the existential threat they faced. The land that we had moved freely upon for generations, that our entire way of life depended on, was progressively shrinking as greedy invaders flooded in without permission, often violently displacing Diné residents and kidnapping and enslaving our mothers, sisters, and daughters.[6] Many of these initial settlers were squatters who held neither legal nor moral title to the land. Diné warriors mobilized defensive actions to protect the land and people from these waves of settler aggression. They were quite successful up until Hwéeldi, a time of great sorrow and suffering for the Diné.

Settlers in New Mexico faced the real possibility of expulsion by Diné forces and complained to the US government, begging the US Cavalry to implement a scorched earth campaign against the Diné. Only a large-scale genocidal military campaign could

---

5 Undated handwritten essay by Thomas Dodge. Arizona State University, Thomas Dodge Papers, Box 7, Folder 23.

6 In the second draft of this note, Dodge struck the phrase "ever increasing aggression" [of the white man] and replaced it with "greedy encroachment."

stop the superior Diné forces and clear the land for settlement by outsiders. The US also wanted to punish the Diné for their effective resistance. Dodge describes the period leading up to Hwéeldi: "In fact [the Navajo] were so triumphantly successful with their far-ranging attacks and pillages of the Mexican settlements and Pueblo villages . . . of the Rio Grande River that it became necessary for the United States to go to war against them in 1863 and to herd and drive them in 1864 to Bosque Redondo as vanquished people deserving no sympathetic consideration except as prisoners of war."[7]

Hwéeldi, or the death march of Diné people known as The Long Walk to Bosque Redondo (present day Fort Sumner, New Mexico) and their internment as prisoners of war from 1864 to 1868, established conditions for permanent settlement by invaders in and around Diné territory. It opened Diné treaty lands to the Santa Fe Railroad to expedite secure passage for settlers and the resources required to make settler occupation permanent. The enduring harm of Hwéeldi is present in the permanent enclosure of the reservation, which limits a people whose very identity is based on freedom of movement in relation to the land. Indeed, Diné still struggle to maintain our way of life on a diminished and often polluted land base; such restriction of space suppresses our ability to thrive. This is perhaps most evident in the catastrophic livestock reduction policy that sought to punish our people for allowing our multiplying sheep herds to "overgraze" our diminished land base, which is entirely consistent with the Diné philosophy of abundance. The message of livestock reduction was that Diné growth should be limited to activities that are "sustainable" within the confines of imposed reservation borders. Meanwhile, settlers enjoy unobstructed growth just across the reservation border (and often within reservation lands via resource extraction) because settler jurisdic-

---

7 Undated handwritten essay by Thomas Dodge. Arizona State University, Thomas Dodge Papers, Box 7, Folder 23.

tion has circled its wagons around Diné Bikeyah, limiting the available space for Diné development.

In other words, settler encroachment never ended, nor did its insatiable appetite for land and resources. It is, as Diné scholar Andrew Curley has argued, "shape shifting," for when our warriors' resistance challenges settler order, it invents new methods of domination to erase and destroy Diné senses of place and home.[8] Today, Indian rolling works in tandem with settler geographies that police our people (and sheep) if they are designated as "off the reservation" or out of place. Any Native person "off the reservation" is fair game for Indian rolling. To be "off the reservation" is to be outside the forced enclosure known as the reservation or the prisoner-of-war camp; it is to trespass into settler territory without permission. From a settler standpoint, those marching in Farmington in that hot summer of 1974 and that September day in 2024 were "off the reservation," as were the three Diné men slain in 1974 and the two Diné men slain in 2014. However, from a Diné standpoint, enclosure is a fiction. After all, how can you trespass on your own land?

And so, Diné resistance continues.

GENERATIONS OF DINÉ GREATNESS

Warrior intellectuals like John Redhouse walk without fear because they possess unflinching clarity about who and what constitutes an enemy. Indeed, there can be no mistake after reading this memoir about who and what the enemy is, what makes them tick, what they are capable of, and where their weakness lies. To study one's enemy is a crucial element of seeking justice, for in that study, one finds a truth that ignites action to stand up and fight for Indigenous freedom, as our relatives did in 1974. The truth is often gruesome and painful, as in the case of those slain by Indian killers. The work of a warrior intellectual, however, is not to catalog the intergen-

---

8 Andrew Curley, *Carbon Sovereignty: Coal, Development, and Energy Transition in the Navajo Nation* (Tucson: University of Arizona Press, 2023).

erational trauma inflicted upon our people by centuries of settler violence. Rather, it is to get the facts straight in the telling of that history—to counter the enemy's inevitable distortions and lies while also equipping the people with the knowledge needed to take strategic action. An elevated study of one's enemy, such as *Bordertown Clashes*, can also generate enlightened resistance precisely because it illustrates how to turn devastation into strength—a unique province of Indigenous resilience. As our understanding of *resistance* to settler violence (not just the violence itself) grows, so too does our courage and fortitude to never back down.

During his speech at the 2024 commemoration event, Redhouse recounted a comment from Norman Patrick Brown, another important figure in Diné resistance during the Red Power era. Brown proudly called the 1974 uprising a "moment of Diné greatness" when our relatives from all walks of life became warriors. Redhouse echoed this, stating that it was a time of "real Navajo power."[9] I argue that moments of Indigenous greatness are not confined to the events that shape them. Rather, they are alchemic; with each moment of greatness, a new thread is woven into the fabric of resistance, making it stronger. The cumulative power of these moments then reverberates across time, providing both a foundation and a wellspring for new generations of warriors to create not just moments of greatness but a robust and resilient infrastructure of resistance that spans centuries and generations.

The generational nature of Indigenous resistance ensures that Redhouse's work remains relevant to our contemporary moment. In a series of interviews I conducted with Redhouse in October 2023 and January 2024, he told me that the warriors of The Red Nation, a Native liberation organization I co-founded in 2014, "are my movement grandchildren."[10] Like those who rose up in 1974, we started

---

9 Redhouse, *Remarks at the Fiftieth Year Commemoration of the 1974 Protest and Boycott of Farmington, New Mexico.*

10 Oral history interview conducted on October 20, 2023 in Pyramid Lake, Nevada.

The Red Nation in response to the murders of the two Diné men on the west side of Albuquerque. The 1974 uprising in Farmington and other key moments of Indigenous greatness and power were specific reference points as we sat down to formulate The Red Nation's identity. This memoir—which Redhouse first self-published the year The Red Nation was founded—directly influenced the foundations of our work. And so, from the very beginning, we have been self-aware of our place as grandchildren within the intergenerational traditions of Indigenous resistance. We have simply adapted our approach to address the specific conditions of our time.

Those present in 1974 called it the "long hot summer." As I recounted at the beginning of my remarks, when we began our fifty-year commemoration march that September morning in Farmington, the fierce male energy of the sun dominated the atmosphere. It was not supposed to be a hot or particularly sunny day. I believe the heat intensified because our march retraced the footsteps of those who rose up during that long hot summer. But then, something curious happened as we approached the end of the march at the Totah Theater. A breeze picked up and clouds started to accumulate in the sky. Soon, the breeze became a steady wind. As the crowd settled into the theater and the speeches began, a chill rolled in on the air, followed by a few almost imperceptible drops of rain.

I had seen this before. In fact, I had seen it many times at The Red Nation actions and events. The weather will not follow the predictable patterns of a forecast. It almost seems to respond to *our* movements and actions on the ground. It is said that when the temperature drops like it did that day, spirits are present. I think these mysterious weather happenings are blessings and acknowledgements from the warriors of old—ancestors—who continue to guide and protect us in the present. I believe it brings them joy when we act without fear and hesitation to stand up for Indigenous freedom because, in so doing, we reinvigorate the essence of who we are.

The gentle rain that falls on these types of gatherings is a female rain because it cleanses and creates a feeling of peace and compassion. And that's just it. To be a warrior isn't to be perpetually angry.

It is not a proclivity towards violence or war for war's sake. Such racist stereotypes of Diné people have been weaponized time and time again to justify further dispossession of our lands and displacement of our people, as in the case of the Navajo-Hopi land dispute.[11] Yes, the road to liberation is long and hot, but when we resist, we remind ourselves and each other of our greatness and of our love for the land and each other. We remember to live in our power and remain always faithful to who we truly are as freedom loving people. We find peace and compassion in being unapologetically Diné.

WAR STORIES

Bordertown Clashes is a Diné war story. Perhaps it is more accurate to say it is a series of war stories recounted first-hand by a warrior on the proverbial and actual frontlines. We do not have many war stories, let alone those that are written with such meticulous detail and moral clarity. The Red Nation, likewise, is a war story. We tell stories so they will be retold to impart important lessons. But we, the warriors, must tell them first and tell them right so that they are remembered correctly without losing or distorting their meaning and intent. This is why written memoirs by warrior intellectuals are so crucial. Yet, they are exceptionally rare. *Bordertown Clashes* is the first of its kind but, I promise, not the last. We in The Red Nation understand what it means to walk this path because of warriors like John. And, when the time comes, it will be our turn to document our war stories for a new generation. With every war story, we recreate ourselves as a freedom-loving people who will never back down.

---

11 David Brugge, *The Navajo-Hopi Land Dispute: An American Tragedy* (Albuquerque: University of New Mexico Press, 1994).

PART I
BORDERTOWN CLASHES

CHAPTER 1
ORGANIZING AGAINST EXPLOITATION

It was mid-morning on September 19, 1972, when a yellow cab dropped me off at the southeast corner of Vassar and Central SE, across from the University of New Mexico campus in Albuquerque. Carrying my ever-present briefcase and snag bag, I stepped onto the main campus and walked purposefully to 1812 Las Lomas NE, where the Native American Studies Center and the Kiva Club were jointly housed in a single-story adobe under the shade of huge cottonwoods. Opening the dark-brown door, I was immediately greeted by the center's secretary, Lena Lujan, a strikingly attractive, vivacious woman from Isleta Pueblo, and James Nez, a quiet laid-back Navajo student from Shiprock. James was a roommate of Larry Casuse and he directed me to their off-campus, high-rise dormitory room on East Grand, just a few blocks away. When I arrived at the dorm room, I found that my old friend Ricky Anderson, a brilliant Navajo civil engineering major from Farmington, was also one of Larry's roommates.

Larry was there when I arrived and after shaking hands, we spent the rest of the day discussing the important issues and work that had brought us together the previous month. Larry was a member of the Gallup-based Indians Against Exploitation (IAE) central committee and he had recently been elected president of the

Kiva Club (KC). Under his leadership, KC had become increasingly active in Native issues both on and off campus. One area of particular focus was IAE's continuing campaign against the exploitive Gallup Inter-Tribal Indian Ceremonial.

After finishing our intense strategic planning session, Larry took me to the airport to catch a plane to Farmington. Before boarding the plane, I was singled out and physically searched for bombs and other weapons of mass destruction. Airport security was obviously alerted by the FBI and state police, who were no doubt following Larry and me earlier that day. In time, we would get used to—in fact, expect—constant surveillance and harassment by the monolithic oppressor. It was just part of the reality of the Indian rights work to which we were committed.

———

The Gallup Inter-Tribal Indian Ceremonial was established in 1922 by a group of local white businessmen to exploit Indian culture and religion. Most of the businessmen were white Indian traders whose main business was buying and selling Indian-made rugs, blankets, and jewelry. The Gallup Inter-Tribal Indian Ceremonial Association had incorporated itself as a private, allegedly non-profit, corporation that staged an annual four-day profit-making event commercializing Native culture and traditions into a tourist attraction. In reality, this non-Indian controlled and operated association was an extension of the Gallup business community.

In 1939, the private membership association also gained "official state agency" status that guaranteed a yearly appropriation from the New Mexico legislature to subsidize "America's outstanding exposition of dances, sports, and arts and crafts." The city of Gallup shamelessly called itself the "Indian Capital of the World," and the Ceremonial was farcically billed as the "Nation's Tribute to the American Indian."

Gallup was also known as "Indian Drunk Town, USA." The non-Indian liquor industry enabled the problem of Indian alcoholism, making illicit, if not illegal, profits pushing its poison, especially during the annual Ceremonial event. The deeply concerned Navajo Tribal Council passed a resolution opposing the "uncontrolled liquor traffic" and the rise of "unhealthy conditions detrimental to the general welfare of the Indians," which "are permitted to grow unchecked" by the bordertown of Gallup. The resolution declared that the tribal council "hereby takes the stand as very strongly disapproving of the participation of the Navajos" in the Ceremonial and "strongly urges the Navajos to withhold their participation" in the event "unless the town" takes steps to remedy "this dangerous situation." The town of Gallup, of course, did not remedy the situation. The town government did not control the liquor industry; the powerful liquor industry controlled the town. Even so, the Navajo Tribe took a strong stand against the Gallup Ceremonial and planted the seeds of future resistance.

Twenty years later, in 1954, a confederation of New Mexico Pueblos also took a strong position against the Ceremonial and boycotted the event. In early 1969, Navajo Tribal Chairman Raymond Nakai officially opposed the Ceremonial Association's request to seek state funds from the New Mexico legislature to finance the planned expansion of its Indian cultural exploitation program. Several months later, a group of Navajo and Pueblo students, who later became known as the Indians Against Exploitation (IAE), publicly leafleted and picketed the annual event. In 1970, IAE, Southwestern Indian Development (SID), Organization of Native American Students, National Indian Youth Council (NIYC), United Native Americans, and the Indians of All Tribes marched and demonstrated against the Ceremonial. NIYC Executive Director Gerald Wilkinson (Cherokee) spoke for all when he declared, "We were not meant to be tourist attractions for the master race."

In early 1971, Navajo Tribal Chairman Peter MacDonald and All Indian Pueblo Council Chairman Benny Atencio formally opposed the Ceremonial Association's request for federal US Economic Development Administration (EDA) funding for a newly proposed multi-million dollar Ceremonial facility on a section of private non-Indian land east of Gallup. The EDA later rejected the association's proposal due, in large part, to regional Indian inter-tribal opposition. Several months later, IAE and SID marched and demonstrated against the exploitive Ceremonial.

———

In early 1972, Gallup Mayor Emmett "Frankie" Garcia orchestrated a non-Indian power move to "take over" control of the management and operation of the Gallup Indian Community Center. For the last twelve years, the center had served as a base for Indian rights activism. In 1961, Gallup Navajo activist and future Gallup Indian Community Center manager Herbert Blatchford Sr. hosted and co-founded the National Indian Youth Council during a historic meeting at the center. Since then, the center had provided effective leadership training and an organizing base for activist groups like NIYC, IAE, and SID that challenged the Gallup power structure. The Indian-directed and -operated center also strongly opposed the Gallup Ceremonial and Mayor Garcia's plans to solicit federal funds for the construction of a token Indian alcoholism rehabilitation facility in Gallup (which, like the Ceremonial, would likely be controlled and operated by non-Indians). As Gallup Indian Community Center Manager from 1963 to 1972, Herb knew that "the city used the Indian's name to secure federal funds and even calls itself the Indian Capital of the World." He also correctly assessed that "Gallup has shown by past efforts that they are incapable of handling an alcoholism program. If they do get federal money to set up such a program, it will be entered into the [the city's] general fund and from then on, no explanation will be given as to how the money is being spent." After the mayor's attempt to remove him from the non-city position of Gallup Indian Center manager, Mr. Blatchford directly addressed the mayor and his city and county allies:

> I am a native of this area, just like Frankie. But we are differ-
> ent. I am not a political advocate. I may not even be a great
> manager. But I have the belief that our people must survive
> and I am here to help them a little bit in surviving. I haven't

seen any of you at this center. You have come here only to take something from us. Let us count who has been helping the Indian. Your father [Ernest Garcia, an Indian trader] gave us the greatest debt we have with that bar [Navajo Inn] he established near the reservation. The attitude that is being displayed here is the same kind that destroyed that town in South Dakota [referring to Raymond Yellow Thunder (Oglala Sioux), recently murdered by a group of white men in the racist bordertown of Gordon, Nebraska and subsequent organizational response by the American Indian Movement]. It could happen here too. I am not going to stand aside and watch my people wounded, castrated, or ignored.

It was commonly known that the Drunk City, USA's Mayor Garcia was a part-owner in the notorious Navajo Inn near the Navajo reservation. After this statement, Herb Blatchford was immediately suspended on unsubstantiated charges and later terminated by Garcia and his cronies.

His replacement was Pauline Sice, a strong Creek woman who grew up in Gallup and who had personally witnessed and experienced the brutal racism and rampant exploitation prevalent in the hostile bordertown. As the new executive director, Pauline also led the center's Model Urban Indian Center Project, which continued to provide necessary direct services to its target Indian population in Gallup and wider McKinley County. In direct defiance of Garcia and his anti-Indian henchmen, she boldly allowed local activist groups, such as IAE and SID, to continue using the center for leadership training and as an organizing base.

One of the participants in SID's 1972 summer youth work program was a bright young Navajo man named Larry Casuse. He had graduated from Gallup High School in 1971 and was home for the summer after his freshman year at the University of New Mexico. Another acquaintance of mine, Nancy Pioche from Farmington, was directing the program. Nancy was a seasoned Navajo activist, veteran of the Ceremonial protest campaigns of 1970 and 1971, and also worked with the Model Urban Indian Center Project.

Both Nancy and Mitch Fowler—experienced Navajo activists and two-year veterans of the anti-Ceremonial campaigns—provided valuable leadership training and organizing skills to the emerging young community leaders, including Larry. In early August 1972, Mitch called a meeting of IAE to begin organizing another campaign to protest the Gallup Ceremonial.

The IAE core organizers included Larry Casuse, Jemez Pueblo activist Phil Loretto and his Navajo wife Darlene, Gallup Navajo activist Iva Palucci, Laguna Pueblo activist and Ceremonial protest campaign veteran Cathy Marmon, and Zuni Pueblo-Navajo activist JoAllan Tsyitee. The fourth annual campaign also received critical frontline support from individual participants in the SID summer youth work program and from hardcore members of the American Indian Movement (AIM) chapters in Denver and Arizona (Tuba City and Dilkon). They had physically stopped a sacred Navajo dance from being inappropriately performed at the 1972 Southwest All-Indian Pow-Wow in Flagstaff (another bordertown $cheme designed to financially benefit Flagstaff businessmen).

The National Guard was mobilized in preparation for another possible "incident," and the city, county, and state law enforcement agencies were also prepared for a direct confrontation with the gathering Red Power forces. Although the showdown never occurred, the organized and united Ceremonial opposition moved on two fronts. In public, the campaign proceeded legally and peacefully as planned. The groups met with Mayor Garcia at city hall to present their demands. One demand was to stop performing the Navajo Yei-Bi-Chei Dance (actually a cheapened fifteen-minute version of the dance) at the Ceremonial. The first Navajo Medicinemen Conference in Window Rock had previously condemned the continued performance of this sacred Navajo dance at the Ceremonial and the Flagstaff Pow-Wow. Navajo Tribal Chairman Peter MacDonald had also condemned the outrageous sacrilege. It was an absolute demand at the 1972 Flagstaff Pow-Wow and was presented as a non-negotiable demand at the 1972 Gallup Ceremonial. As expected, Plan A did not work. The arrogant mayor leaned back in his oversized chair and refused to consider the demands, saying they were "rather late and rather ridiculous." Larry and I then met with Ceremonial Association Executive Director Edward "Ike" Merry at the Ceremonial grounds but he too refused to consider our demands. Time for Plan B.

That night, as Tom Bee and XIT played at an IAE fundraising concert at Manuelito Hall in Gallup, a secret underground guerilla resistance movement quickly went into action. A direct action here and a direct hit there—some reported, some not—took place over the next four "frenzied" days and nights. In the end, the IAE and AIM's shock troops had succeeded in physically preventing the scheduled performance of the Navajo Yei-Bi-Chei Dance at the 51st annual Gallup Ceremonial. The second major battle victory in two months against two enemy cities had been secured and was part of history. The larger red war against white racism and exploitation continued.

———

It was the last weekend of the 1972 New Mexico State Fair in Albuquerque. For the previous two weekends, members of IAE and the Kiva Club had set up and manned an information booth at the entrance of the fair's Indian Village. They had gathered more than a thousand signatures on a petition opposing the Ceremonial Association's plans to relocate the Ceremonial to a section of private non-Indian land near the Navajo community of Church Rock. The Church Rock Chapter had already passed several resolutions in opposition to the proposed move. Larry Casuse, Phil and Darlene Loretto, Cathy Marmon, JoAllan Tsyitee, and I were operating the booth for the fair's last weekend. We were also allowed to speak directly to the vendors and visitors at the Indian Village, so Larry, Phil, and I spoke passionately against the exploitive Ceremonial and the racist bordertown of Gallup.

The following weekend, we set up our booth at the Northern Navajo Fair in Shiprock and continued to gather signatures for the petition. After the Shiprock Fair, weekly information and strategy meetings were held at the UNM Native American Studies Center.

Also attending and participating in the meetings were Kiva Club student activists Larry Emerson (Navajo), Fred Martinez (Santa Clara Pueblo-Navajo), Ken "Tom Snag" Peyketewa (Zuni Pueblo), and June Toledo (Jemez Pueblo).

In early October, AIM Denver chapter leaders Vernon Bellecourt (White Earth Chippewa) and Rod Skenandore (Blackfoot), who were with us during the 1972 Ceremonial action, led the southern route of the Trail of Broken Treaties Caravan through Gallup and Albuquerque. Representatives of IAE, Kiva Club, and the Albuquerque-based NIYC supported the Indian car caravan to Washington, DC.

We submitted our 1,600-signature petition and supporting documents to the New Mexico Legislative Finance Committee in early October. In our letter of submittal, we also asked the committee to reject the Ceremonial Association's request for state funds for the 1973 Ceremonial. After our signed petition was presented to the finance committee, Larry Casuse asked me to research the power structure of the Ceremonial for the group.

He had already talked to Phil Loretto and requested that we meet in the Gallup-Window Rock area to discuss the research and the finances to support the research. IAE still had a little beso left from the XIT fundraising concert in August. Phil's brother-in-law, Sammy Keams (cousin of Navajo AIM activist Leroy Keams, who was part of the 1972 Flagstaff Pow-Wow action), later picked me up at the Gallup Indian Center and we went to Window Rock, where Phil was working as an architectural draftsman for the Navajo Tribe. Phil told me that we were first going to a speaking engagement at Navajo Community College (NCC) in Many Farms that evening.

We talked about the research on the way to NCC and on the way back to his log cabin at "the summit" between St. Michaels and Ganado. I spent the night with him and his wife, Darlene (who was originally from Dilkon). The next morning, Phil cut me a check for $200 from the IAE bank account and drove me to Yah-Ta-Hey Junction so that I could catch a ride back to Farmington. I generally didn't hitchhike on an empty stomach, so I had a cup of coffee, a bowl of beans, and some fry bread (breakfast of champions) at the little café at JB Tanners before getting on the road. Larry had worked at that little café as a weekend cook during the summer of 1972.

My research revealed that the Ceremonial Association executive director, Ike Merry, was also an Indian arts and crafts trader and, in fact, was the secretary of the United Indian Traders Association. The traders controlled the Ceremonial, particularly the exhibit hall with its lucrative arts and crafts sales. I also learned that the City of Gallup recently appointed a planning committee to work with the Ceremonial Association on plans to jointly develop and operate a permanent multi-facility complex east of Gallup. The planned complex would be anchored by the new Ceremonial grounds and Ceremonial Association office; it would be built on a section of private non-Indian land recently purchased by the association. The construction and operation of the proposed complex would be based on a Joint Powers Agreement signed between the Ceremonial Association and the City of Gallup. This agreement would establish a Joint Powers Commission—jointly appointed by the association and the city—as the complex development and management entity.

I also dug into related issues, such as the jurisdictional implications of the checkerboard land ownership pattern surrounding the 640-acre Red Rock site and the potential effect of a major wrongful death lawsuit recently filed by survivors of a non-Indian accident victim against the Ceremonial Association and possible liability for the State of New Mexico.

Additionally, I dug into other issues related to Gallup city mayor and Navajo Inn part-owner Emmett Garcia—there was a recent resolution passed by the St. Michaels Chapter against the continued operation of the Navajo Inn, a petition signed by local Navajo citizens opposing the current liquor licensing status of the Navajo Inn, a public and private nuisance lawsuit filed by local tribal residents against the owners of the Navajo Inn (the ABA Corporation), and the issuance of excess liquor licenses in Gallup, the Gallup Interagency Alcoholism Coordinating Committee, Gallup Alcohol Abuse Rehabilitation Design, and the McKinley Area Council of

Government. The research was then analyzed and used largely for strategic purposes.

In early November, the Kiva Club, led by Larry Casuse, traveled to Seattle and established a strong student presence at the fourth annual conference of the National Indian Education Association (NIEA). JoAllan Tsyitee, an IAE Central Committee member, also attended and participated in the conference. She was a teacher at Laguna Pueblo Elementary School and served on the First American Task Force of the National Education Association (NEA). After a week of intense lobbying and strategic campaigning by Larry, JoAllan, and the Kiva Club, the NIEA finally passed a resolution opposing the Gallup Ceremonial. The National Indian Education Association joined other national Indian organizations in opposing the annual event, including the National Congress of American Indians, National Indian Youth Council, United Native Americans, and the American Indian Movement. At the conference, the Kiva Club also networked with other student organizations and convened the Southwest Regional Caucus meeting that established a Southwest Indian Student Coalition. The next meeting of the Coalition would be held at the Gallup Indian Center before a scheduled march and demonstration by IAE and the Kiva Club on Thanksgiving Day. Protest activities on this National Indian Day of Mourning (or Unthanksgiving) would be directed at the hypocritical Ceremonial. In the words of Larry Casuse, the theme and message of the action would be "Thanks for Nothing!"

After playing a couple of games of pool at the Gallup Indian Center, Larry, Phil, and I met in the center conference room the day before the Southwest Indian Student Coalition meeting. We finalized the agenda for the two-day meeting and then prepared for our next meeting with the city and state police to complete the logistics for the scheduled march and demonstration. The eight-mile march would begin at Church Rock Indian Village on the morning of Unthanksgiving Day and proceed south and west to the Ceremonial Association office on US 66, where we would then hold a rally with speeches and demonstrate with picket signs. After the rally, we would march back to the Indian Center and the center staff would host a big feast. The final logistics meeting with the city and state police went quite well and we were now ready.

They came from the four directions. They represented Indian student organizations from most of the major universities and colleges in the Southwest. In addition, there were student group delegates from Navajo Community College, College of Ganado, Southwestern Indian Polytechnic Institute, and the Institute of American Indian Arts. They met in a circle for two days and, operating by consensus, they effectively advanced the work that had started in Seattle. The second day of regional coalition building and youth empowerment ended with a prayer and a commitment to meet again in the spring of 1973. Then, in a strong show of support and solidarity, most of the students chose to stay and join us in our march and demonstration the next day.

The following morning, over 250 Native people gathered at Church Rock Indian Village and began the eight-mile march to Gallup. We marched along the frontage road north of Interstate 40, handing out leaflets to the drivers who stopped and requested copies. Then, without warning, the state police arrested Diana Beyal, a fourteen-year-old Navajo resident of Church Rock, for leafleting. When Mitch Fowler intervened on her behalf, he too was arrested for interfering with an (unlawful) arrest. Both arrests were clearly unconstitutional. The march proceeded along the frontage road, under the I-40 overpass, and along Route 66 to Boardman, where the marchers turned south and marched directly to the city police station where Diana and Mitch were illegally held. As angry marchers surrounded the building, we met with the police chief and began arranging for the release of the two unjustly arrested and detained political prisoners. We also called and left a message with DNA People's Legal Services in Window Rock, which had assisted in our legal protest against the Ceremonial in August. We then marched north on Boardman to 66, where we resumed our march to the Ceremonial Association office. After a brief rally and picket sign demonstration, we marched back to the Gallup Indian

Center, where Pauline Sice, Lillian Malone (Navajo), Josephine Quiver (Navajo), Albert Quiver (Oglala Sioux), and other center staff members were waiting for us with a huge feast.

Afterward, the IAE Central Committee debriefed at Cathy Marmon's sister's trailer in West Gallup. Committee members Cathy and JoAllan Tsyitee had driven from Albuquerque to participate in the march and demonstration. The next day, IAE spokesman Larry Casuse issued a strong statement to the press: "We were armed only with a drum, signs, and our minds against the police force armed with shotguns, pistols, and billy clubs. And they arrested a fourteen-year-old girl for stepping on the pavement of the great state of New Mexico."

We met with the Ceremonial Association's Indian Involvement Committee in Gallup in late November and early December to discuss our recent position paper on the Ceremonial and its recommendations. Unfortunately, the committee of Native people did not seriously consider, much less address, the merits of our substantive proposal for positive and constructive change. So, the thing that happened was that nothing happened. We wanted solutions and alternatives, but they didn't. They had no ideas, only criticism of ours. Well, at least you can't say we didn't try. Depressing as it was, Ike Merry's song-and-dance men—hopeless cultural exhibitionists— would rather keep on dancing for the white man's pennies than actively pursue true Indian self-determination.

Giving up on the so-called Indian Involvement Committee, we focused our attention on Emmett Garcia, who was recently appointed as Chairman of the Gallup Interagency Alcoholism Coordinating Committee (GIACC). Phil and Larry asked me to write up a fact sheet on this latest outrage and a petition calling for Garcia's removal as GIACC chairman. I, of course, was only too happy to do so. The fact sheet described the Navajo Inn controversy and questioned the legal issuance of excess liquor licenses in Gallup. It also discussed the high incidence of alcohol-related traffic accidents on New Mexico State Road 264 near the Navajo Inn and the tragic history of Navajo and Indian alcoholism in Gallup.

The petition was straightforward, basically calling for the "rejection" or de-appointment of Garcia as chairman. He was a large part of the problem, so how could he be part of the solution? As a "successful" second-generation package liquor store business partner, he was probably not going to divest his ownership interest in the Navajo Inn, the cesspool on New Mexico State Road 264, because it was also part of his inheritance. As mayor, he wasn't interested in doing anything politically or legally to revoke the excessive liquor licenses issued and operating in Gallup. The non-Indian liquor industry controlled Indian Drunk City, USA and obviously he was not the right person to chair GIACC. It was more than a positional conflict of interest—it was part of a larger hypocritical business operation that was killing Indian people here and at this very hour and that was unacceptable.

As the petition against Garcia circulated, we met as individuals (rather than as a group) in mid- and late-December. Right before Christmas, I met with Larry at his mother's house in Gallup. After our meeting, we watched my beloved Oakland Raiders play the hated Pittsburgh Steelers on black-and-white TV. I was devastated by the last-second "Immaculate Reception" and game-deciding touchdown by Steeler rookie Franco Harris. Still devastated, I went to Farmington and met with Mitch Fowler and Navajo activist Penny Hunter, then to Bernalillo to meet with Phil Loretto. The petition against "Dammit Emmett" (as he was now called) continued to circulate.

In early January 1973, Phil joined the staff of the Model Urban Indian Center Project at the Gallup Indian Center. He assisted IAE and the Kiva Club members who testified at a public hearing protesting the racist funding scheme to celebrate the Anglo-American Bicentennial. The public hearing was held in Gallup by the New Mexico Bicentennial Commission. In mid-January, the New Mexico Legislative Finance Committee recommended a zero appropriation to the Ceremonial Association for the Ceremonial. This recommendation to the state legislature was largely based on the petition and supporting documents that we had submitted to the committee in

October. After considering an unwise proposal to sue us and the 1,600 valid petition signers, the Ceremonial Association renewed its request for state funds and began lobbying the New Mexico legislature at its annual session in Santa Fe. In a related development, the Joint Powers Agreement was co-signed and executed by the City of Gallup and the Ceremonial Association. Signing for the city was Mayor Garcia. Signing for the association was board president and Gallup businessman Jay Vidal (who supported the earlier proposal to sue us "to prove a point"). The agreement was then submitted to the State of New Mexico for final approval.

At an IAE press conference in late January, we offered support and explanation for the reasons motivating the recent armed protest at the US Indian Health Service hospital in Gallup by six members of the American Indian Movement. We later joined AIM Denver chapter leader Vernon Bellecourt and members of the AIM Fort Defiance chapter at the arraignment of the six AIM protesters in Gallup. By early February, the IAE Central Committee continued meeting in Gallup and Albuquerque on the weekends. We were also following AIM and AIM-affiliated group activities in Custer, South Dakota and on the Pine Ridge Sioux reservation. We also supported the reasons behind the previous AIM-led takeover of the US Bureau of Indian Affairs central office in Washington Deceit.

———

At the beginning of the spring semester in 1973, Larry Casuse moved out of his off-campus, high-rise dormitory room on Grand NE and into a rented house on Park SW with Larry Emerson, June Toledo, Fred Martinez, and Tom Snag. Larry began dating a young Sioux woman, originally from South Dakota, who worked as a nurse at the Gallup IHS hospital. She described the criminal conditions at the hospital, and helped Larry understand the reasons behind the AIM members' recent armed protest. He also developed a better understanding of the reasons for AIM's direct confrontation with the police riot squad in the white racist bordertown of Custer and the desperate living conditions on the Pine Ridge Sioux reservation in South Dakota that later led to the liberation of Wounded Knee.

I began dating JoAllan Tsyitee. Her grandfather was a Zuni Pueblo from Zuni Pueblo south of Gallup. Her grandmother was a Navajo from LA (Lupton, Arizona). They met as students at the Albuquerque Indian School. After they graduated, they married and her grandfather worked at the school for forty years until he retired. JoAllan was born in Albuquerque and later raised by her grandparents until she graduated from Valley High School in Albuquerque's North Valley. She then attended and graduated from the University of New Mexico, where she became a member of the Kiva Club. When I met her at the IAE information booth at the New Mexico State Fair Indian Village in September 1972, she was a teacher at Laguna Pueblo Elementary School and a member of the First American Task Force of the National Indian Education Association.

When we began dating in early February 1973, she told me about the ongoing Zuni Pueblo campaign to reclaim Zuni Salt Lake in western New Mexico and Zuni Heaven in eastern Arizona. She also told me about the Pueblo's early efforts to establish its own school district, separate from the racist Gallup-McKinley County School District. I had spoken at the new Ramah Navajo High School on the Ramah Navajo reservation, east of Zuni Pueblo, in McKinley County in the fall of 1970, and knew a number of the progressive Navajo faculty and staff members. In fact, I had met most of them during the 1970 Ceremonial protest. JoAllan and I were both familiar with the 1971 study "An Even Chance: A Report on Federal Funds for Indian Children in Public School Districts" and the related case of *Natonabah v. Board of Education of Gallup-McKinley County*. So, we had plenty to talk about, making our special relationship even richer.

———

In a bizarre move, New Mexico Governor Bruce King nominated Emmett Garcia to the Board of Regents of the University of New Mexico. Garcia was not even a college graduate but apparently had strong local and regional political influence in the state Democratic Party. The Kiva Club and IAE mobilized to lead an intense campaign opposing the nomination. In mid-February, the groups rallied at the State Capitol in Santa Fe to protest Garcia as a member of the UNM Board of Regents. We also lobbied against the Ceremonial Association's renewed request for state funds at the annual session of the New Mexico legislature. In addition, we met with the state Legislative Finance Committee, the Department of Finance and Administration, and the Commission on Indian Affairs directed by former Kiva Club member Joe Herrera (Cochiti Pueblo).

In late February, Larry Casuse and Phil Loretto testified against Garcia's nomination at a hearing of the New Mexico Senate Rules Committee. Larry presented our revised petition statement and fact sheet opposing Garcia as both the chairman of the Gallup Interagency Alcoholism Coordinating Committee and a proposed member of the UNM Board of Regents, stating, "We feel that Emmett Garcia is not qualified to become part of the UNM Board of Regents. A member of the regents should be a man of prestige in his community. Emmett Garcia does have the prestige. How he obtained it is what we question. Yet, he ironically is chairman of the Alcohol Abuse Rehabilitation Committee. Does he not abuse alcohol? Does he not abuse it by selling it to intoxicated persons who often end up in jail or in a morgue from over-exposure?" Nevertheless, the heartless Senate Rules Committee recommended confirmation of the nomination, and the equally heartless New Mexico Senate confirmed the nomination.

Back on campus, the Senate of the Associated Students of the University of New Mexico overwhelmingly passed a resolution condemning the appointment and a rag doll of Emmett Garcia was burned in effigy. The *New Mexico Daily Lobo* published a strong editorial rejecting Garcia's appointment. The Kiva Club and a broad-based coalition of student organizations held a mass rally on the university mall and then marched to Scholes Hall to protest the swearing-in ceremony of Emmett Garcia as a new regent. Larry directly addressed the Board of Regents and spoke about the corrupt political nomination and appointment process:

> These are the type of people who run our government, and these aren't The People—these are false people. There's no reason for me to scream and shout. There's no reason for me to bring documents. There's no reason because you people will just turn your head, like you always turn your head. There's no reason for that. So what we're going to do is, we're going to find all the human beings in this country, in this state, and we're going to get the human beings together and we're going to put an end to people like Emmett Garcia, and we're going to start with Emmett Garcia. We don't really care what you people do. Because you people aren't human beings.

After Larry's statement, the Board of Regents swore in Emmett Garcia. With so much of our attention diverted to the Garcia matter, we only later learned that the Joint Powers Agreement had been approved by the New Mexico Department of Finance and Administration and the state Board of Finance. We also learned, after the fact, that the Ceremonial Association's renewed request for state funds was approved toward the end of the legislative session as part of the amended general appropriations bill for fiscal year 1973–74.

The last time I saw Larry was on a cold Sunday afternoon in late February when he dropped me off on the side of Interstate 25 outside of Albuquerque so that I could hitchhike north. I had run out of operating money and was broke.

———

On February 27, the armed liberation of Wounded Knee by members of the Oglala Sioux Civil Rights Organization and the American Indian Movement began. Two days later, Larry Casuse and Robert Nakaidinae (a young Navajo man from Fort Defiance and a cousin of Michael Upshaw, one of the AIM protesters who had occupied the Gallup IHS hospital in January) went to Gallup and put Emmett

Garcia under citizen's arrest. Garcia later escaped from custody by kicking Robert in the leg when he was not looking and then breaking through the front door window of the sporting goods store where he had been detained. The city and state police then fired rounds of bullets and tear gas into the building, so Larry and Robert returned fire. Larry was wounded by enemy fire and Robert surrendered so that Larry could be helped. Several eyewitnesses said that the fatal gunshot was fired *after* Robert surrendered and police had entered the building. A short time later, police dragged Larry's body out on the sidewalk.

I heard the news late that afternoon and made my way down to Gallup with help from my good friends Greg Cajete (Santa Clara Pueblo) and Ramona Coriz (Santo Domingo Pueblo). Early the next morning, I met with Phil at the Gallup Indian Center. This was a crisis situation, and we had to show strong leadership (even though both of us were only twenty-one years old). First, we met with Larry's mother and family in Gallup. Next, we met with the Indian Center staff and issued a public call for a community meeting at the Indian Center the following day. On March 3, the other members of the IAE Central Committee, Kiva Club, Southwest Indian Student Coalition, AIM, and other Indian and non-Indian allies arrived. Soon, the Indian Center was packed—at least 1,500 Navajos, Pueblos, Apaches, Utes, and members of other tribes—and more were coming. Phil and I co-facilitated the gathering. Larry's father, Louis from Mexican Springs, spoke eloquently of his son's brave sacrifice; June Toledo's father, Jose Rey Toledo from Jemez Pueblo, addressed the overflowing crowd with great dignity and power; National AIM leader Herb Powless, an Oneida from Milwaukee, gave a fiery speech; and Cecil Largo, a Navajo community leader from Standing Rock who had witnessed the March 1 incident, recounted what he saw and heard in somber detail. There were other powerful speakers who spoke with courage and iron strength and whose gifted oratory and sacred wisdom brought out the best in us on that sad and angry day in Gallup.

We had already met with the city manager and police chief at city hall to obtain a permit to march through downtown that day. We marched from the Indian Center to Stearn's Sporting Goods Store, where Larry was killed, and then to Rollie Mortuary, where Larry's body lay. From the mortuary, we marched back to the Indian Center. Phil and I addressed the marchers, and the daylong gathering ended peacefully. The IAE Central Committee held an internal group meeting in the Indian Center conference room before we all returned home or went back to Albuquerque.

Phil, Darlene, and I went to Albuquerque that evening so that we could meet with the Kiva Club the next day. The state police followed Phil's red Volkswagen Beetle all the way to LorLodge on East Central, where we stayed for the night. The following morning, we ate breakfast at the Frontier and then met with the Kiva Club Council and other club members at the Native American Studies Center. This was the first time I met with the council; in fact, it was the first time I met with most of the Kiva Club members. After introducing ourselves, Phil and I spoke and then answered questions. A productive discussion followed and we soon agreed to work together in the future as there was still unfinished business with Emmett Garcia. Before returning to Gallup, Phil, Darlene, and I met in private with Larry Emerson, June Toledo, Fred Martinez, and Tom Snag at their house on West Park.

On March 5, we met with Larry's family at Rollie Mortuary and assisted with the logistics of the funeral, memorial, and burial of our dear friend and brother. Four days had passed and it was now time for him to return home to rest in honor with Manuelito, Barboncito, and the other great Navajo warrior chiefs who also led their people in fierce battle against the enemy invaders. Larry would be buried at Mexican Springs, where his father Louis still lived. Larry had taken me to his father's home in August 1972, only seven months earlier. Now, we were taking him back home to Nakaibito.

We helped organize the funeral procession from the mortuary and the Gallup Indian Center to Mexican Springs. Over two thousand people attended the services, including Navajo Tribal Chairman Peter MacDonald. At the gravesite, Larry Emerson gave a stirring eulogy in Navajo. Then Phil spoke. And then I. An eagle circled overhead as we and the other pallbearers laid Larry down into the ground. A light snow fell and, in the distance, a rainbow appeared over Chuska Peak. After the reception, a long car caravan returned to the Gallup Indian Center, where Larry Emerson, Phil, and I addressed the mourners. Among the mourners were Navajo high school seniors Elva Benson and Shirley Martin, who led student walkouts at Gallup High School and Tohatchi High School to attend the funeral earlier that day. We later learned of another student walkout at Tuba City High School.

During this crisis period, the IAE leadership received specific death threats from persons unknown. I suspect that some of them came from redneck scum in the liquor industry after the bars in Gallup were ordered to close for public safety reasons for several days following the March 1 firefight and subsequent Indian response. Otherwise, the bros under the influence would have torn up the town. But as good as that sounded, it would have eventually led to a one-sided massacre and the killing of a lot of Indian people. As usual from the other side, there were some poorly disguised agent provocateurs—posing as instant Indian revolutionaries—who tried to recruit us to "avenge" the death of Larry Casuse. Although it had a certain appeal, we had never seen any of them before and we didn't trust them. It was obviously a COINTELPRO-styled setup, and we weren't going to play into their hands. Besides, it would have been impossible to get to Emmett Garcia at that time because he was too well guarded by the Indian-killing cops.

Phil continued to work with the Gallup Indian Center and the Model Urban Indian Center Project and I worked mainly with the Kiva Club, mostly on weekends. In late March, the Kiva Club and IAE organized a large march from the university down Central to Robinson Park, where a rally was held in honor of Larry Casuse and in support of Robert Nakaidinae and the continuing occupation at Wounded Knee. At the same time, the Kiva Club and the Native

American Studies Center kept the pressure on the UNM Board of Regents and Governor Bruce King to remove Emmett Garcia and appoint a qualified Indian regent (with at least a college degree) in his place. Then, in a rather strange move, which seemed more political than business, Mayor Garcia invited IAE, Kiva Club, and the Gallup Indian Center to meet with him about the future of the Navajo Inn at city hall. We met with him, but he didn't have much to offer. Our demand on the Navajo Inn was quite clear—close it down immediately and permanently and retire the liquor license. He was not willing to do that because the Navajo Inn "has steadily been the single most profitable liquor store in the state of New Mexico."

This meeting (or rather the appearance of a meeting) may have been politically motivated since Garcia was running for re-election against challenger Sam Ray, a city councilman from the anti-Garcia North Side. Ray was no friend of the Indian, but at least he was not as bad as the incumbent mayor. We didn't really care about bordertown politics because it's always been pro-exploitation and anti-Indian. Nevertheless, the non-Indian-owned Navajo Inn was strategically located near the border of the dry Navajo reservation; its sole purpose was exploiting the deadly disease of alcoholism— Navajo alcoholism—for maximum corporate profits. Therefore, in the spring of 1973, we determined that it was necessary to remove Garcia from his positions as mayor, Gallup Interagency Alcoholism Coordinating Committee chairman, and UNM Board of Regents member. He was our Public Enemy Number 1 because he was dangerous as a politician and a businessman. If we could stop him by mobilizing the sheer will and power of the People and summoning the collective human spirit, then we, the People, had the moral obligation—indeed the imperative—to try.

We sent out the word. There would be a march in Gallup on March 31 bigger than any march in the town's history. It would be a People's March for Mother Earth, Father Sky, and Humanity. It would be a march in remembrance and honor of Larry Casuse. It would be a march in support of Robert Nakaidinae and the liberation and continued occupation of Wounded Knee. We would march west from the old Ceremonial grounds, south across the bridge, railroad tracks and Route 66, east on Coal through downtown, and north and east back to the Ceremonial grounds, where we would then present our demands to the City of Gallup. Larry Emerson asked me to write the demands. I wrote twenty demands, mostly concerning the removal of Emmett Garcia and the closure of the Navajo Inn. Kiva Club member Louise Four Horns (Navajo) typed them up on the brown IBM Selectric at the Native American Studies Center and we made a thousand double-sided copies at the UNM student copying center.

For the next two weeks, we didn't sleep. We just organized. The night before the march, Kiva Club leaders Glen Paquin (Laguna Pueblo), James Nez, and I went to Grants and met with the directors of the Gallup Indian Center and Model Urban Indian Center Project, Pauline Sice and Michael Benson (Navajo), to review last-minute logistical and security details. The next morning, we met at the Gallup Indian Center, which served as a communications center for the upcoming March 31 event. Several of us were also able to talk by phone with Robert, who was incarcerated in the maximum security section of the Gallup gulag. Soon, it was time to march, and march we did—over three thousand of us—deep into the belly of the beast. There were heavily armed and extremely dangerous city, county, and state police, paramilitary SWAT squads, and snipers on every building rooftop downtown, helicopters flying overhead, and the activated and fully mobilized National Guard units. Still, we marched, wave after wave of red, brown, black, and white humanity. Marching in unity and beauty—men, women, children—all singing the AIM song. On this day, we had come to town and we had shut it down.

We finally returned to the old Ceremonial grounds and waited for the last marcher. Then, great people spoke—Larry Emerson, Jose Rey Toledo, Navajo activist and future tribal leader Peterson Zah, Navajo tribal spokesman Chester Yazzie, Charles Becknell, Fred Ward, and many others. A telegram of support from Wounded Knee also arrived, signed by AIM leaders Russell Means (Oglala

Sioux), Dennis Banks (Leech Lake Chippewa), Clyde Bellecourt (White Earth Chippewa), and Carter Camp (Ponca). The twenty demands were then read and presented to acting Gallup mayor Sam Ray, who said that the city would officially respond to them in the very near future. Emmett Garcia was reportedly out of town.

Two days after the march, I personally met with Governor Bruce King at his office in Santa Fe and reconstructed the history of regional Indian intertribal opposition to the Gallup Ceremonial. He had claimed that he was not aware of Native opposition to the event when he signed the amended general appropriations bill for FY 1973–74 that re-funded the Ceremonial. I then met with Legislative Finance Committee staff director Maralyn Budke and Deputy Director Waldo Anton about the Joint Powers Agreement. Mr. Anton informed me that the agreement had been declared unconstitutional by the state attorney general but that the City of Gallup and the Ceremonial Association were in the process of "making it legal." Finally, I met with Commission on Indian Affairs director Joe Herrera and chief executive staff assistant Delores Chandler about the legally dubious dual status of the Ceremonial Association as a state agency and a private non-profit corporation. They too questioned the legality of the quasi-state agency.

———

On April 3, the walls began tumbling down. In a major upset, Emmett Garcia was defeated by Sam Ray. No longer mayor, Garcia soon resigned as chairman of the Gallup Interagency Alcoholism Coordinating Committee and then from the UNM Board of Regents. He moved out of his hometown of Gallup and to Pinetop, Arizona. The native son would not return home to live. The Navajo Inn closed and was later demolished. Garcia's political career was destroyed forever and his life's business interests lay in ruins east of Tse Bonito.

Despite these victories, IAE was not the same without Larry Casuse. We stopped meeting as a group. Phil Loretto and I still met but more as individuals than as members of a group. He later resigned from the Gallup Indian Center. In June, we held an IAE benefit concert with XIT, Paul Ortega (Mescalero Apache), and Joe JoJola (Isleta Pueblo) at Manuelito Hall. The funds raised helped Phil and his family move to Durango so that he could attend Fort Lewis College. He was our intellectual and was deeply missed.

I was still dedicated to the original IAE cause and continued to work with the Kiva Club on weekends until the end of the spring semester. I primarily worked with Glen Paquin, James Nez, Junella Haynes (Cherokee), Aviva Kempner, Klara Kelley, JoAllyn Archambault (Standing Rock Sioux), and other members of the newly formed UNM Gallup Study Group to develop models for summer student research on the power structure of Gallup and McKinley County. Aviva and I also worked on the legal defense for Robert Nakaidinae and the six AIM protesters who occupied the Gallup IHS hospital in January.

Aviva, Don Devereux, and I also raised funds from several foundations for IAE to continue and expand its scope of work in Gallup and on the Navajo reservation. After the funds were raised, I served as IAE Summer Projects Coordinator in Gallup from early June to mid-August. One of our projects was the Church Rock Project, in which we employed five local Navajo students—Kee Yazzie, Ron Hudson, Geraldine Thomas, Yvonne Dixon, and Diana Beyal— to work with their affected community and the Navajo Tribe on the Ceremonial issue. I also served as an adviser to the Gallup Study Group.

In July, IAE, Kiva Club, Gallup Indian Center, and the Gallup Study Group met twice with Gallup mayor Sam Ray and the city council about our revised demands but faced opposition to the demands related to the Ceremonial, Joint Powers Agreement, Joint Powers Commission, and the proposed Red Rock multi-facility complex project. We knew that they would oppose those demands so we decided to continue working directly with the Church Rock chapter and the Navajo tribal government, which both supported our strong position.

In July and August, the 1973 Flagstaff Pow-Wow and the 1973 Gallup Ceremonial were both canceled.

Two more victories! What a way to end the summer!

CHAPTER 2
THE LONG HOT SUMMER OF 1974

After carefully packing the beaded turquoise necklace Navajo college student Karen Dixon made for me in the early spring and the white calypso shirt my Jewish friend and colleague Aviva Kempner gave me for my twenty-second birthday in July, I was finally ready to gallop out of town and head for the bright lights of Albuquerque to attend the University of New Mexico. It was the last day of my summer work project and a week before registration for the beginning of the fall semester. I was excited and feeling good. My girlfriend, JoAllan Tsyitee, had returned from her summer graduate school studies at Arizona State University in Tempe and was waiting for me in the big city. A week of nightclubbing in the Duke City with JoAllan and Cathy Marmon followed—I had a lot of catching up to do. Then it was time to hit the books.

After student registration and getting my GI Bill, Navajo tribal scholarship, and a full tuition waiver, I got a nice apartment on Sycamore SE, close to Jack's, Okie's, and, oh yeah, the university. Zuni Pueblo-Navajo student activist Marley Shebala nominated me to the Kiva Club Council, and I began using the Native American Studies Center and its significant resources as a base for my continuing activist work. I quickly got to know or know better the center staff, the Indian studies faculty, and most of the Kiva Club members. I continued my work with the Robert Nakaidinae Legal Defense

Fund, the Gallup Ceremonial and Red Rock State Park issues, and other issues, including the Navajo coal gasification controversy, Tucson Gas and Electric (TG&E) case, and the Exxon uranium lease matter. Additionally, I began working with the Kiva Club's American Indian History Project coordinated by Glen Paquin. JoAllan and I also renewed acquaintances with Phil Loretto and Iva Palucci, who were both attending college and doing well—Phil in Colorado and Iva in Arizona. UNM graduate and former Kiva Club member Cathy Marmon was busy working in the new family business on North Fourth. Although the IAE Central Committee no longer existed, its surviving former members were getting on with their lives but never forgetting the turbulent events of the past year.

Politically and socially, my life was full. Academically, I did just enough to get by. I would always start the semester with eighteen credit hours, then drop to fifteen, and finally down to twelve— the minimum for a full-time student—by the end of the semester. When I actually went to class, I would use the time to draft a press release or compose demands instead of listening and taking notes. Fortunately, I mostly took easy courses and when I had to, I promptly made up my incompletes during the semester break so that I could maintain my higher education funding and other valuable assistance like tuition waivers. I did, however, learn how to use the university library system, not so much for my classes as for my work-related research. The Zimmerman Library, law library, business library, and engineering library allowed me to do important government, legal, corporate, and technical research. At the law library, I was also able to interact with the American Indian Law Center and the American Indian Law Students Association.

I also changed my method of operation as my situation stabilized. First, I had an apartment that I used as my home base. Before, when I was working with the Kiva Club on weekends from early March to mid-May, I slept at the Native American Studies Center. A long-tenured Kiva Clubber showed me how to get in and out of the center without a key. And when I began working in Gallup from late May to mid-August, I just crashed in my office or on one of the couches at the Indian Center. That was okay with center director Pauline Sice.

Secondly, I stopped hitchhiking—JoAllan made sure of that. My old hitchhiking circuit was Farmington, Gallup, Window Rock, Albuquerque, and Santa Fe. Now, with Albuquerque as my new base, JoAllan drove me where I needed to go—mainly on weekends since she worked during the week and I was supposed to be going to school. She also took me to Laguna Pueblo and other pueblos for their dances and feasts. In December, we went to Zuni Pueblo for Shalako. The all-night ceremony was a powerful experience and one that I will never forget.

In January 1974, I drafted a major funding proposal and a letter of transmittal for the Gallup-based Diné Bi Tsi Yishtilizhii Bii Cooperative to finance the expansion of its arts and crafts training program. I had worked as a part-time consultant for the Gallup Business Development Center in May to write a business plan for the cooperative and later employed Navajo activist Art Neskahi to work with the cooperative and its training program as part of the IAE summer work project from June to August. The grant proposal and transmittal letter were finalized and submitted to the Four Corners Regional Commission in Farmington.

In early February, cooperative director Louise Largo (Navajo) and I met with the new Ceremonial Association director, William Ganong, and the board of directors in Gallup to secure a resolution opposing the proposed issuance of $4 million in tax-free bonds from the City of Albuquerque to Sunbell Corporation of Albuquerque to help finance the planned expansion of a factory that "mass-produces machine-made imitation Indian jewelry." We approached the Ceremonial Association because, as a state agency, it was legislatively charged with the responsibility to help preserve and protect Indian arts and crafts or Indian-made arts and crafts. Our initiative was part of a larger statewide Indian campaign against Sunbell and the fake Indian jewelry industry. Facing a united Indian front, the non-Indian corporation soon withdrew its application for city bonds.

Later that month, the Kiva Club met with Gallup mayor Sam Ray to request that bars in the city close on March 1 in honor of the First Larry Casuse Memorial we were organizing in Window Rock. We also asked Mayor Ray to speak at the memorial. Ray said that he "individually" supported our request for the city bar closure and that he would speak at the memorial event. The Gallup bars, of course, did not close on March 1 and Sam Ray did not honor his promise to speak at the memorial. In fact, he didn't even show up. But several hundred Native people, including Russell Means and Dennis Banks, did show up at the Navajo Civic Center for the day-long memorial. Besides Russell and Dennis, Navajo AIM leader and Wounded Knee veteran Larry Anderson also spoke. Then Navajo nationalist and future tribal councilman Fred Johnson delivered an unforgettable speech on the true meaning of ultimate sacrifice and the warrior's code of no surrender. Following Fred, Navajo elder Lenora Collins from Iyanbito and many others who came on this day of remembrance also spoke from the heart. The memorial ended with the AIM song resonating throughout the full auditorium. The next morning, JoAllan and I visited Larry Casuse's grave at Mexican Springs.

———

Sarah Platero from Bluewater also served on the Kiva Club Council, which flourished under her strong leadership. She was a Navajo pre-law major and a Wounded Knee veteran. I had been following the Bureau of Indian Affairs takeover cases and the prosecution of the Custer and Wounded Knee defendants, including AIM leaders Russell Means' and Dennis Banks' national speaking tour to raise funds for their legal defense. Thanks to the hard work and activist leadership of Sarah and the Kiva Club Council, Russell and Dennis were coming to UNM to speak at the Student Union Building Ballroom. The national AIM leaders also met with the Kiva Club and other local supporters at the Native American Studies Center before and after their standing room–only speeches. Inspired by the speeches and meetings, an AIM Albuquerque chapter soon formed with Lena Lujan and Tom Snag among the new chapter leadership.

After the speeches, I met with Navajo activists Fred Johnson, Wilbert Tsosie, and Al Henderson. I already knew Fred and Wilbert from Farmington, and I was working with Al on the TG&E and Exxon issues since they affected the lands of his family and extended family. I also met with Americans for Indian Opportunity leader LaDonna Harris (Comanche) after the speeches to discuss the recent Sunbell controversy and the need to strictly enforce the federal Indian Arts and Crafts Board Act in the future.

A Native daughter of Canyon De Chelly, Penny Hunter, was also a member of the Kiva Club and a co-founder of the Diné Coalition that was working with Burnham chapter president Eva Arthur and other local Navajo residents on the coal gasification issue. As members of the Kiva Club Council and the Diné Coalition, Penny and I were also co-coordinating the Kiva Club's Navajo Coal Gasification Project. Along with Navajo activist and former IAE summer work project employee Elvira Burnside, we worked with the UNM Navajo Reading Center to develop community education materials on the gasification issue. We also formed a truth squad to "crash" campus presentations by coal gasification and mining company representatives. In addition, we sponsored a major forum on the Navajo coal gasification issue at the Aquinas Newman Center across the street from the Native American Studies Center. I served as facilitator of the forum. The forum panelists were Western Coal Gasification Company representatives Al Paisano and Herbert Tsosie, El Paso Natural Gas Company reps Charles Hunter and Allen Gleason, Navajo tribal executive staff assistant Andrew Benally, and DNA People's Legal Services attorney Robert Strumor of Shiprock who was working with a number of Navajo community residents opposed to coal gasification and mining in their area. Tom Campbell of the Central Clearing House in Santa Fe also showed his new film documentary, *Look at What They've Done to this Land*, which featured legendary Nenahnezad grandmother and coal mining opponent Emma Yazzie. The well-attended forum

49

produced lively discussion and sharp debate between the presenters and the participating audience. Putting a cap on the forum, UNM and Kiva Club alumni Omar Bradley (Cherokee) said, "Now coal gasification is officially on the table."

—

Navajo Tribal Chairman Peter MacDonald was the keynote speaker at Kiva Club's annual Nizhoni Days, a week-long cultural and educational event. I talked with the chairman for about twenty minutes before his speech at the anthropology building lecture hall. First, I thanked him for attending Larry Casuse's funeral. I also thanked him for publicly supporting the reasons for the 1972 BIA takeover. I always liked his nationalism and his genuine hatred for the Bureau. Since we disagreed on the environmental problems of coal gasification, TG&E and Exxon issues, we didn't talk about those subjects. Instead, we discussed the Navajo land claims case and tribal water rights. He then gave me some good legal and technical referrals that I would later follow up. His keynote speech gave special recognition to the Kiva Club for its long proud history, tradition of strong leadership, and advocacy on important issues. A masterful speaker, he touched on a wide range of subjects, from fighting white apartheid in Apache County to strengthening tribal governments and economies to engaging in nation-building and tribal development opportunities. In closing, he declared tribalism a valid way to live in the twentieth century and challenged the Native students to be effective members of their tribal communities.

JoAllan was soon going to DC for her quarterly NIEA First American Task Force meeting. It was fortunate that I could join her on this trip and follow up on some of the referrals from Chairman MacDonald. Aviva Kempner met us at the airport, and we spent the first night at her apartment in Dupont Circle. She was in her first year of law school. The next day, JoAllan attended her task force meeting and Aviva ditched school to take me to meet Indian water rights attorney Bill Veeder and hydrologist Phil Corke at the BIA central office. Phil wasn't there but I had a great meeting with Bill and his longtime secretary, Inez Miller. They loaded me up with legal documents and offered to send more in the mail. Bill also suggested that I meet with Dr. Phil Reno at the Navajo Community College Shiprock Branch for more detailed information on Navajo water rights. Aviva then took me to the National Congress of American Indians (NCAI) office on Connecticut and later to the Library of Congress and the National Archives.

Afterward, we hooked up with JoAllan and went to Angie's Gardens on the north side, where we had a delicious Italian dinner. I was pretty small-town then and didn't even know what house wine or house dressing were. Before Angie's, my idea of fine dining was eating at Mucho Burger in Gallup or having one of those blue-plate specials at the Woolworth's luncheon counter in downtown Albuquerque.

After dinner, Aviva took us on a walking tour of Georgetown, then across the Francis Scott Key Bridge into Virginia and back again. On M Street, we went up the steep steps to the house where *The Exorcist* was filmed. As we were looking at the dark spooky house, some crazy teenagers drove by yelling, "Raay-gaan!!" At that point, we decided to call it an evening and went down the Father Karras steps to the street. From there, Aviva caught a cab back to her apartment and JoAllan and I flagged a taxi to the Gramercy Hotel, where the rest of the task force members were staying. The next morning, JoAllan went to her second day of meetings while I stayed in the hotel room to study the documents Bill and Inez gave me. It was my first trip to Washington, and I had learned a lot that would prove quite useful in the months and years ahead.

When I got back to ABQ, I realized that I had forgotten to return a film projector I had borrowed from the university. As I was walking up East Gold to return the projector, a cop stopped me and accused me of burglarizing a local neighborhood house in broad daylight and ripping off a home projector. I calmly corrected him and told him to follow me to the university if he wanted to. Of course, he declined. After returning the projector, I dropped by University Drugstore and had a fountain soft drink. My next stop was the law school library to check out the Navajo tribal land claims documents (Docket 229) that Chairman MacDonald had referred me to. It was such a nice day that I thought I would walk—across Central, up Yale, across Lomas, up Yale again, and past the medical school to the law school.

I had never seen the actual Navajo land claims map before but when I did, I took special note of the historical and geographical fact that the white racist bordertowns of Gallup, Farmington, and Flagstaff were illegally located on aboriginal Navajo lands—stolen tribal property that was unconstitutionally taken by the US government without monetary compensation or fair and just payment. I later met with Navajo tribal land claims attorney William Schaab of the Rodey et al. law firm located downtown to obtain additional history and background on the tribal land claims case and get an update on the pending docket. Schaab had also been the lead attorney in the successful Taos Pueblo Blue Lake case and campaign. I told him that Chairman MacDonald had referred him and mentioned that I visited Taos Pueblo in 1969 and had listened to a memorable speech by Taos Pueblo leader Paul Bernal at the height of the Blue Lake issue. After our meeting, Bill Schaab loaded me up with more legal documents that I hauled back to my already-document-cluttered apartment. I was developing quite a library then—documents, periodicals, files, and books. JoAllan didn't seem to mind. She even bought me a special newspaper clipper for my stacks of yellowing, dog-eared *Gallup Independents* and other bordertown dailies.

For her birthday, I took JoAllan to the Shanghai Chinese Restaurant for some dim sum. There, we met my old friend Conroy Chino (Acoma Pueblo). I had known Conroy since our NIYC days in 1969–70. He was now working as a reporter for KOAT-TV and wanted to interview me and our old NIYC buddy Charlie Cambridge (Navajo) for a special half-hour television program on the state of the Indian rights movement. Charlie and I agreed to the thirty-minute interview. The following week, we had the interview—with Conroy as the host and Charlie and I as the guests. It went very well. At the time, Charlie was directing NIYC's Job

Recruitment Program and told me to apply for a summer student internship with Wilbert Tsosie, another NIYCer from the old days who was working as the Indian Projects Coordinator for the San Juan County Economic Opportunity Council in Farmington. I applied to the council's director, Ken Rustad, with Wilbert's hearty recommendation and got the internship. I had known Wilbert since the early sixties but we didn't tell Ken that.

Charlie and Wilbert were primarily responsible for me—as a graduating senior at Farmington High School—applying to attend NIYC's Clyde Warrior Memorial Institute in American Indian Studies at the University of Colorado in Boulder in the summer of 1969. I was accepted, and that's where I met Conroy, Cathy Marmon, and my other NIYC brothers and sisters from around the country and Canada. Conroy later went on to become Kiva Club president and led the Indian student campaign to establish the Native American Studies Center.

———

Toward the end of April, newspapers reported the recent discovery of the mutilated bodies of three Navajo men north of Farmington. The men had been brutally beaten, tortured, and murdered. At that time, there were no suspects. Wilbert called me and said that he would try to find out more information on the murders and leads to possible suspects. I shared this conversation at a special meeting of the Kiva Club Council. On April 28, Wilbert called again and told me that three of the suspects had been arrested and that they were white teenagers from Farmington. He also asked me to organize a major press conference in Albuquerque on the racially motivated hate crimes. The next day, Larry Emerson and I contacted the media and scheduled a press conference for the following day at the Native American Studies Center. On April 30, we held the press conference that included representatives of the Kiva Club, Native American Studies Center, AIM Albuquerque chapter, and NIYC. Larry, myself, NASC director Harvey Paymella (Hopi-Tewa), Tom Snag, and Gerald Wilkinson all made strong statements condemning the racist murders and demanding swift and full racial justice. After the press conference made statewide news, Wilbert called me and said that we should also hold a major press conference in Farmington to keep the issue alive and the pressure on. I went to Farmington that evening to help him organize the press conference. Wilbert picked me up at the bus station and we talked and strategized all night on the bluffs south of Farmington.

The next morning, we went to Wilbert's office at the San Juan County Economic Opportunity Council and began organizing. First, we reserved the Farmington Indian Center for the press conference and a public meeting, which were scheduled for that evening. We also finished up my paperwork for the summer student internship, which would begin the week after the end of the spring semester and end the week before the beginning of the fall semester. I would be sharing the second-story corner office with Wilbert. I also met several of his co-workers, including the agency's legal aid attorney Howard Graham and the Reverend Billy Cleaver, who was also president of the Farmington Chapter of the NAACP. When asked about his last name, Billy confirmed that he was distantly related to the Black Panther Party revolutionary Eldridge Cleaver. I also ran into Reverend Henry Bird of the San Juan County Human Rights Committee. I had met the San Juan Mission Episcopal priest in 1972 and again in 1973. In fact, he sent a letter and a check to forward to the Robert Nakaidinae Legal Defense Fund in March 1973.

Since the three white teenage killers were Farmington High School students, our next meeting was with the school's assistant principal, Barry Sigmon, and local youth leader Dennie Kripokapich. I had known Barry when he was a social studies teacher at the high school and we had talked a couple of times about local Indian issues after I graduated. I also knew Dennie's father, Bosko, who worked as a federal grants officer at the Four Corners Regional Commission (which was reviewing a funding proposal for the Diné Bi Tsi Yishtilizhii Bii Cooperative to expand its arts and crafts training program). During our meeting, Barry shared some information about the student killers and Dennie showed us a petition that he was circulating among the rest of the student body that strongly condemned the killings of the three Navajo men. There were actually quite a few signatures on the petition and I thanked him for his remarkable leadership initiative and fine work.

We then went to city hall to obtain a parade permit for a memorial march for the three Navajo men. We planned a downtown march to take place on Saturday, May 4. I filled out the parade permit application, which was quickly approved, and we planned to announce the march at the press conference and public meeting. That evening, the Indian Center was packed and emotionally charged. I facilitated the press conference and Wilbert facilitated the public meeting. Participating in the evening events were Wilbert, myself, AIM national treasurer Larry Anderson, Navajo professional and Farmington Intertribal Indian Organization board president Dr. Bahe Billy, Navajo tribal vice chairman Wilson Skeet, Navajo grassroots leader Lucy Keeswood, and many others. Speaking in English and Navajo, Wilbert announced the march on Saturday and gave directions. Larry also announced that AIM had set up a camp at his uncle Jimmy's residence in Shiprock, and he and his uncle Jimmy would organize a volunteer party to search on horseback for other bodies of Navajos in the area north of Farmington, where the first three bodies were found.

After the public meeting, I spoke with Alma Arnold of the local NAACP on the need to work together to fight white racism in Farmington (the Selma of the Southwest). I remembered her and her two sons from growing up on the poor side of town where most of the Indians, Blacks, and Mexicans lived. I also talked briefly with local assistant district attorneys Byron Caton and Tom Hynes, who were charged with prosecuting the three white teenage killers. The two white prosecutors did not think the Indian killings were racially motivated. I later found out that Mr. Caton had represented the family of one of the Indian killers when he was in private practice. Of course, he didn't see that as a conflict of interest in his present prosecutorial duties and remained on the case.

The next day, we prepared for the march—logistics, security (our own security guards with red bandanas and armbands), lists of speakers before and after the walk, and other program details. Word of the march was out, and Wilbert's office was suddenly transformed into an organizing headquarters. While we were busy organizing, coffee shop rumors started by local white reactionaries started flying. Soon, the press was calling every five minutes asking us to confirm the "report" that a DC-3 with AIM written on it had landed at the Farmington airport. The "threatened" white folks in Farmington were apparently wetting their pants, so Economic Opportunity Council attorney Howard Graham had us speak at a luncheon of the apparently influential Church Women United as a last-minute rumor control measure. I'm not sure we allayed any rumors but at least we got a public forum and a free lunch. In the afternoon, we received information from the AIM camp in Shiprock that there would be a thirty-mile march from the camp to Farmington along New Mexico State Road 550 (known as Slaughter Alley due to the driving while intoxicated-related deaths) and that the marchers would hold protests at the Turquoise Bar in Hogback and the Zia Bar in Fruitland on their way to join the march in Farmington. We were also informed by Navajo community organizer Andy Beyale that there was a car caravan from Counselor, Nageezi, and Huerfano driving to Farmington on State Road 44 (the Ribbon of Death, again due to the DWI-related deaths) and the participants would hold protests at several non-Indian owned package liquor stores in Lybrook on their way to join the Farmington march. The march was taking on a life of its own—in a good way! That evening, JoAllan called me and said that she would be driving up to Farmington early the next morning to be part of the People's March. She was a real trouper.

On May 4, the Indians came to town. From the west, from the south, from the east. Thousands came. Larry Emerson estimated four thousand. They gathered at the northwest corner of Broadway and Lake. Wilbert Tsosie and Fred Johnson addressed the gathering, speaking in English and Navajo, they explained the purpose of the memorial march. Then, the march began, led by the widow and children of Herman Benally, one of the three Navajo men killed by the three white teenagers. The youngest child carried a sign that read, "Herman Benally was my father." The people marched to Main Street and proceeded east toward downtown. It was a silent march of remembrance and respect for the deceased men. It was a deeply powerful march for justice.

As they marched through downtown with handmade signs, there were police riot squads stationed at every corner and paramilitary snipers posted on the rooftops (much like Gallup on March 31, 1973). Still, the People marched with respect, courage, and dignity. Following Rena Benally and her children, the People turned south on Orchard and then west on Broadway. They marched back to the gathering place, four thousand strong, united, respectful. Then the People spoke—Wilbert, Fred, Lucy Keeswood, Phillip Yazzie, Larry Anderson, Lorenzo LeValdo, Andy Beyale, Dick Charley, and many, many more. "We will no longer be silent," the People said, "We will march in the streets again and again and again until we have justice."

The day after the march, JoAllan and I went back to Albuquerque and talked about our plans for the future. Her school year would be over at the end of the month, and then she would take several summer courses at UNM for her teacher's license certification renewal. I would move to Farmington for my summer internship at the Economic Opportunity Council (EOC) and stay at my parents' home which was only three and a half blocks from the office. After the internship, I would move back to Albuquerque for another academic year at UNM. She would return for another school year at Laguna Pueblo Elementary. On a personal level, we planned to move out of our apartment on Sycamore at the end of May and find a bigger place closer to the university. We also planned to get married in June and then get away for a week for our honeymoon.

During the final exams week at UNM, I did what I had to do to keep my eligibility as a continuing full-time student for financial aid and tuition waivers. In fact, I would rate my spring semester as an academic success—I passed all my classes with no incompletes to make up.

In the real world, we still had to organize—finals week or not. In addition to our extracurricular campus organizing and mobilization, Larry Emerson and I convinced the university's Associated Students Senate to unanimously pass a resolution strongly condemning the recent hate crimes in Farmington. We also got the student government body to modify its budget to include a special appropriation to charter several university buses for students to attend the next march in Farmington.

Per our summer plan, JoAllan and I would go up to Farmington for the march. After the march, she would drop me off at my parents' house for the summer (or at least most of it) and drive back to Albuquerque. But as it turned out, the three-month plan didn't work out quite that way.

The May 11 march would allow the People to present their demands to the city government. They had formed an umbrella group called the Coalition for Navajo Liberation (CNL) which consisted of the Farmington Intertribal Indian Organization, San Juan County Human Right Committee, Farmington NAACP chapter, AIM, Kiva Club, and a number of concerned Navajo individuals such as Fred Johnson, Al Henderson, Harris Arthur, Claudeen Bates Arthur, and others. Larry and I represented the Kiva Club. At the first meeting, held at the San Juan Mission overlooking the racist bordertown of Farmington, CNL had written ten demands to present to Mayor Marlo Webb (or "Spider Webb" as the local Navajos called him).

The march on May 11 began at the gathering place and proceeded east on Broadway toward downtown. After protesting in front of the notorious Esquire package liquor store (strategically located a block from the Indian Center), the marchers turned north on Orchard and then west on Main Street, walking past the racist Sambo's Restaurant to Smoak Chevrolet (of which the mayor was part owner). After protesting the "unscrupulous" car dealership, the marchers turned north on Airport Drive, walking past Basin

Lodge (owned by assistant DA Tom Hynes' family), up the hill past city hall, to the southwest corner of Municipal and Navajo, next to the heavily fortified police station, and below the National Guard Armory on Airport Hill. The police and National Guard were, of course, fully mobilized against the unarmed marchers.

It took a lot of courage for our people to march in the mean streets of Farmington, where the white crazies would just as soon kill you as look at you. Unarmed, brave were the marchers, the thousands of marchers, and on that day, they went en masse to see the mayor. Wilbert read the ten demands to Marlo Webb, who received them on behalf of the city. Webb tried to joke, saying that he felt like Custer surrounded "in a sea of Brown faces." One of the demands called for a meeting between the Coalition for Navajo Liberation and the mayor and city council to "seriously consider" the other demands, which ranged from a truly Indian-directed and operated Indian Center to the establishment of an alcoholism rehabilitation facility. Then Fred Johnson announced that CNL would continue to march in the streets of Farmington to keep the pressure on until the city responded to their demands. Fred was followed by Lucy Keeswood, Mary Wallace, Waldo Emerson, Clarence Tsosie, Sr., Jimmy Anderson, Victor LeValdo, Sylvia Cambridge, Don Lee, Charley Toledo, Bert Mescal, and many other Navajo elders and youth who had come to town to march for justice.

On May 13, I began my summer student internship. On paper, Wilbert Tsosie was my supervisor and my vaguely defined project was titled "Indian Lifestyles in a Reservation Bordertown." My project committee, also on paper, consisted of Fred Johnson, Bahe Billy, Bosko Kripokapich, and Phil Reno. The internship was perfect cover for a summer of full-time organizing. Plus, I had company. Al Henderson's wife, Elva Benson, was also a summer student intern at the Economic Opportunity Council supervised by Howard Graham. I had known Elva since 1972 when she was a member of Southwestern Indian Development in Gallup. She was also a member of the National Indian Lutheran Board and later helped secure an emergency grant for IAE during the crisis period following the murder of Larry Casuse. A Shiprock native, she was now home for the summer after her freshman year at Yale University.

Two days after the march, Mayor Webb and the city council members held a listening session at McGee Park Auditorium to hear grievances from the Indian community. It was clear that the city had no intention of acting on the many concerns presented; in fact, the mayor said as much when he told the presenters that the city officials were there to listen but not to act. It seemed to be a vast waste of time.

Two days later, Indian community members met with Gerald Wilkinson, John Dulles II, and Gustavo Gaynett at the San Juan Mission. Mr. Wilkinson was the NIYC executive director and a member of the New Mexico State Advisory Committee to the US Civil Rights Commission. I had known Gerry since 1969 when we met at NIYC's annual organizational meeting in Albuquerque. We also worked together on the recent Sunbell issue. Mr. Dulles represented the Southwestern Regional Office of the Federal Civil Rights Commission. I had met John in Albuquerque in February to discuss reimbursement for IAE's work with the Commission on the 1973 Navajo civil rights investigation and hearings held in Window Rock. Mr. Gaynett represented the Community Relations Service of the US Justice Department. I didn't know Gaynett but heard that he was in Gallup in March 1973. The six-hour meeting with Gerry, John, and Gus was highly productive in terms of fact-finding and amassing evidence for the preparation and filing of future individual and group civil rights violations complaints.

A week after AIM had begun searching, the decomposed body of another Navajo man was discovered "floating" in the San Juan River west of Farmington. The family of the deceased man had reported him missing. It was likely that more bodies were yet undiscovered. Based on the large number of missing local Navajo persons, there had to be a literal boneyard of hate crime victims in the greater Farmington area.

As the killing fields continued, the People continued to march in downtown Farmington. The Saturday marches on May 18, 25, and

June 1 each drew several thousand people, mostly Navajos. Black and white members of the local NAACP and the San Juan County Human Rights Committee also participated in the weekly marches.

Surprisingly, JoAllan drove up every weekend to join me in the marches and rallies. Not surprising, however, was the fact that I had not done any work on my summer student internship project. All of my time at EOC was spent on organizing and agitating. As the Saturday marches continued, the downtown businesses continued to suffer and soon the suffering businessmen called on the city to "do something" about the peaceful, legal marchers. The police riot squads and rooftop snipers were apparently not enough. After five marches without a major incident and with no end in sight, something had to be done to really provoke or intimidate us.

On June 3, we applied for a parade permit to march on Saturday, June 8 but were told that the San Juan County Sheriff's Posse had already applied for a permit to hold its annual parade downtown that same day and that its application was already approved.

Since our parade permit was denied, Wilbert and I then went back to the EOC office and talked at length with California photojournalist Bob Fitch, who had covered the civil rights marches and demonstrations in the Deep South in the sixties. Bob took great pictures of our last march and the minor confrontation with the police riot squad that was trying to intimidate us with its latest show of force. Bob came to town around the same time we burned the mayor in effigy at the city dump between the third and fourth marches. That media event received good press coverage and soon a parade of reporters came in from *Time, National Observer, New York Times, Washington Post, National Catholic Reporter, Rocky Mountain News, Albuquerque Journal, Durango Herald, New Mexico Independent, Santa Fe Reporter, Seers Catalogue,* and other publications. After Bob left, I returned a call to Tom Barry of *Seers Catalogue* (an alternative newspaper published in Albuquerque's North Valley) and arranged an interview.

It was almost noon, so Billy Cleaver and I went downstairs to eat at Jean's a couple of doors down. We were boycotting nearby

Sambo's for obvious reasons. Over spicy meatloaf and mashed potatoes and gravy, Billy asked what I was going to do on Saturday since we were not permitted to march. Chewing thoughtfully on a buttered dinner roll, I told him that JoAllan was coming up for the weekend and that we would probably just housesit since my parents were going to Boulder to visit my sister and her family. After leaving a generous tip for the friendly Navajo waitress, I went outside and glared at white racist Sambo's up the street. Only a few weeks before, the segregationist restaurant had refused to serve the Navajo members of the new special tribal civil rights commission established by Navajo Tribal Chairman Peter MacDonald to address the very problem of racial discrimination in the mayor's city. Back at my office desk, I could still see Sambo's across the street. There was no escape. Finally, after shutting the window blinds, I started work on my summer student internship project. Most of the rest of the bye week went by slowly.

———

It was finally Friday and I thought it would be another slow day. But before the day was over, it would become a Day of Infamy. Shortly after nine o'clock in the morning on June 7, EOC legal secretary and Navajo CNL member Lucille Mesa informed Wilbert and me of an urgent phone call from Rena Benally, the widow of Herman Benally, who was one of the three Navajo men killed by the three white teenagers. Wilbert took the call and talked with Rena for about ten minutes. After they finished, he slowly set the phone down and told me that she had called from a phone booth outside the San Juan County Courthouse in Aztec. Rena and the other two widows and surviving families of the Navajo men were not allowed to attend a court hearing, which was proceeding behind closed doors. So, Wilbert and I told Lucille that we were going to Aztec to find out what the hell was going on.

When we arrived at the county courthouse, we surveyed the situation. There were about 150 Navajos outside and a bunch of heavily armed white men from the county sheriff's office guarding the locked doors. We immediately began raising hell. Soon, Assistant District Attorney Byron Caton came out and met with us. He said that the new state juvenile code prevented the public and the press from attending the court proceedings. He then told us that he was "trying like hell to get these guys bound over to adult court" and to "please have faith in the system." Well, the system failed miserably, as we heard on the news that evening that the three confessed murderers were given a slap on the wrist by a white district judge from Gallup. They were sentenced to the state boys' reform school at Springer until they turned twenty-one or earlier. If three Navajo teenagers had killed three white men in San Juan County, they would have all been given the electric chair if they were not lynched first. That evening, we learned that the families of the three confessed murderers were allowed to attend the court hearing in Aztec.

The next day, I was at my parents' house, waiting for JoAllan, when Wilbert came by to tell me that there was a nineteenth-century cavalry unit in the Sheriff's Posse Parade approaching downtown as we spoke. Wilbert and I met up with Lorenzo LaValdo and Navajo CNL member Taft Scott on the south side of Main Street across from the Allen Theater. We briefly discussed the matter and decided to physically stop the parade by standing in front of the horse-mounted cavalry unit that was about a block away from us. It was the right thing to do.

First, the city denied our permit to march for racial justice so that the white sheriff's posse could have their pro-cowboy, anti-Indian parade. Secondly, a white bordertown judge gently slapped the wrists of the three white savage killers with lenient sentences of a few easy years at the state boys' reform school. And now, the sheriff's posse brings in the armored National Guard from Fort Bliss with a six-man cavalry unit. When I think of the cavalry, I think of their swords slicing off the breasts of our women and throwing babies in the air then impaling them with their bayonets, Kit Carson's roundup, his scorched earth policies, and the forced Long Walk to Bosque Redondo.

So, we did what we had to do. They charged at us and we took their best shot. They threw tear gas and we threw it back—a strong gust of wind blew the tear gas back towards the mounted cavalry and their horses reacted as horses will when tear gas fills their nostrils. The police tried to throw me through a plate glass window but I did a quick judo move and it was two of them that went through the plate glass window. But, in the end, there were too many of them— city police, National Guardsmen, sheriff's posse. Thirty-one of us were arrested on that day, but at least we stopped the parade and, in stopping the parade, we stopped the advance of the racist cavalry unit. Sometimes, you have to stop racism with your bodies.

JoAllan and EOC attorney Howard Graham got me out of jail the next day. The media was waiting outside the police station and the first one to interview me about the riot on Main Street was Conroy Chino from KOAT-TV. After the interview with Conroy, we went down to the San Juan Mission where over a thousand supporters, including Larry Anderson, were gathered. They all cheered when they saw me and I returned their cheers with a strong Red Power fist salute. For an activist, there is no better feeling than that—knowing that you have that kind of support from real people. Although Lorenzo was the ringleader in stopping the parade, he somehow managed to escape arrest and was safely back on the rez. So, I met with Henry Bird, Billy Cleaver, and Howard Graham on trying to get Wilbert, Taft, and the others out of jail.

Eventually, everybody got out and we were arraigned on various misdemeanor charges before city judge Roy Marcum, a former Farmington police officer and a former San Juan County Sheriff. After pleading innocent to the false charges, our trial dates were set. Prosecuting the cases was city attorney Dwight Arthur. Wilbert and his sister Dorothy, however, faced additional charges—felony charges—for allegedly assaulting the rioting police. They were later arraigned on the additional charges in state district court in Aztec. The assistant district attorney prosecuting their cases was Tom Hynes.

After the Farmington arraignment, JoAllan and I went back to Albuquerque for the rest of the week. We then met with several criminal defense attorneys, including Charles Driscoll, who defended Chicano land grant activist Reies Lopez Tijerina for his role in the famous 1967 Tierra Amarilla Courthouse Raid (the Chicano Wounded Knee). After the meetings, it was clear that we still needed to raise more money for both legal fees and expenses.

Because we rained on the sheriff's posse parade, the city filed a motion for an injunction in state district court to enjoin us from freely exercising our constitutional right to march. The state court in Aztec granted the city's motion. Acting as a private citizen, Fred Johnson then filed a motion for an injunction in state district court to enjoin six white-owned "Indian bars" in Farmington and San Juan County from operating as public nuisances. In his motion, he specifically charged that the bars illegally sold liquor to already intoxicated Navajos, making them easy prey for hate crimes.

Although we were enjoined from marching on June 15, we did participate in the First Navajo Nation Unity Days in Shiprock. It was a positive, four-day alternative event happening at the same time as the Gallup Ceremonial and organized by Larry Emerson, Tom Snag, Al Henderson, Elva Benson, Iva Palucci, and other individual and organizational members of the new Coalition for Indians Against Exploitation. I was involved in the initial planning of the Shiprock event but only had time to do some quick research for a pamphlet, which Larry later produced. The alternative event allowed the People to boycott the Ceremonial by attending a truly Indian-conceived and controlled cultural event on an Indian reservation.

Calls for a Navajo boycott of Farmington were a major theme in our bordertown campaign. Even mayor and businessman Marlo Webb acknowledged our potential economic power, admitting that the Navajo dollar is the difference between profit and loss in Farmington and the non-Navajo business community knew that. To help us realize our economic power, Larry brought UNM reservation economic development professor Richard Wilson (Santee Sioux) to the Shiprock chapterhouse to explain how Indian boycotts of racist and exploitive bordertowns have worked elsewhere. Richard cited the case example of Bemidji, Minnesota, where the surrounding Red Lake, White Earth, and Leech Lake Chippewas successfully boycotted the anti-Indian town and forced it to its knees. In fact, he said the town mayor was literally on his knees begging the tribes to lift the boycott. The tribes, of course, had demands and after their demands were met, they conditionally lifted the boycott. This inspired Fred, who then met with the Cortez and Durango Chambers of Commerce; they promptly agreed to lower their business prices for his group. He later organized a group shopping trip to Durango while maintaining his principled boycott of Farmington.

We still did not have individual or group legal counsel for our various criminal and civil cases (except for Fred's citizen suit). Fortunately, though, Wilbert's father, Clarence, knew through his social work a friendly and helpful woman named Carmie Lynn Toulouse, who was the daughter of James Toulouse, a well-known Albuquerque civil rights attorney. Carmie Lynn talked to her father, who immediately agreed to represent us pro bono in our various cases. He had a high-powered law firm and assigned another daughter, a lawyer, Charlotte Mary Toulouse, and two other attorneys, Leonard DeLayo, Jr. and Kent Winchester, to assist him in representing us. I first saw Jim Toulouse in action at a preliminary hearing in the Tsosie cases before state district court judge Clement Koogler in Aztec and was highly impressed. He moved easily from criminal defense to civil rights law, convincing the federal district court in Albuquerque to declare the state court injunction against us unconstitutional. The city appealed. We challenged their appeal. Ultimately, we won the right to march in the streets of Farmington again. Every time we won a smashing legal victory, we held a major press conference at the NIYC national headquarters in Albuquerque. The press loved it because we were always the underdog.

While we were kicking their unconstitutional rumps in court, we had a couple of adversarial meetings with the mayor, city council, and their white Mormon-led Navajo Relations Committee. The far-cical committee collapsed in a heap after one meeting. We also had a hostile meeting with an arrogant representative from the state in Shiprock. Fred finally had to tell the visiting state head, "If you disre-spect my people one more time, I will personally kick your ass." The warning must have worked because the state rep didn't disrespect the Navajo people for the rest of the meeting. Appropriately, Fred's statement headlined the front page of the *Albuquerque Journal* the next morning. The earned respect continued as Fred and Wilbert were later bestowed the honorary titles of Colonel Aide De Camp by Governor Bruce King at a follow-up meeting with the state in Santa Fe.

Armed with a federal court order, we resumed our weekly downtown marches in Farmington. JoAllan and I also helped organize a large CNL march in Albuquerque, from the University of New Mexico, down Central, to Robinson Park, where several hundred marchers rallied.

We also revised some of our demands. At a press conference before the Albuquerque march and rally, we specifically demanded that the US Civil Rights Commission hold public hearings in Farmington or we would "issue a national call for continuous demonstrations in Farmington each day of the month." Within a month, the New Mexico State Advisory Committee to the federal Civil Rights Commission held three days of public hearings on the status of Navajo civil rights in Farmington. We participated fully in the hearings and subsequent investigation. Within a year, the committee submitted *The Farmington Report: A Conflict of Cultures*, which validated in whole what we had said and done during the long, hot summer of 1974.

CHAPTER 3
WORKING FOR A GREATER INDIAN AMERICA

After carefully packing a beautiful purple velvet shirt and a brand new pair of black cowboy boots gifted to me by CNL leader Lucy Keeswood, I headed down the trail to Albuquerque. A few hours earlier, I had whipped out an acceptable research report for the San Juan Economic Opportunity Council that met the minimum requirements for my summer student internship project. The nineteen-page report wasn't my best work, but it was good enough to earn my last weekly project stipend. Those weekly stipends had subsidized my summer organizing in Farmington, ultimately serving the greater good. It was a good thing that Wilbert Tsosie was my project supervisor and Fred Johnson was one of my project advisers. JoAllan and I got married in Santa Fe in July and found a nice two-bedroom apartment close to the university on Vassar SE. One of the bedrooms was reserved for my office and library. Everything seemed good.

Then, things changed—again. A week after I registered as a full-time student for the fall semester, National Indian Youth Council executive director Gerald Wilkinson offered me the position of NIYC associate director. I accepted his offer on the condition that I would attend school full-time and work part-time for the 1974–75 academic year. Then, after the spring semester, I would work full-time and forget about school for a while. JoAllan didn't like it. She thought that I should finish my undergraduate studies and then go to law school. After law school, then I could work for a group like NIYC as a lawyer. As she put it, the issues would still be there. In the interest of maintaining marital bliss, I told her that I would decide at the end of the spring semester. Actually, I had already decided what I would do but just didn't tell her that at the time. In the meantime, I would go to school full-time and work part-time until mid-May 1975. The first thing I did, though, was drop from eighteen to twelve credit hours.

The day after Labor Day 1974, I began working part-time as NIYC associate director. I made sure to schedule my classes in the morning so that I could work in the afternoon and evening. When I started work, Charlie Cambridge and the other staff members of the organization's Job Recruitment Program had already left. Although the successful program was not re-funded by the BIA, it did establish a solid track record that allowed NIYC to apply for a prime sponsor designation under the federal Department of Labor's new Comprehensive Employment and Training Act (CETA) to serve all off-reservation Indians in the State of New Mexico.

NIYC consisted of Gerry, two secretaries, and an alternative high school program housed next door, directed by Ramona Wilgus (Hopi), and funded by the Albuquerque Public School District. When I started, Gerry, myself, and the two secretaries—Verna Williamson (Isleta Pueblo) and Theresa King (Navajo)—were paid out of a $30,000 general support grant from the Field Foundation. However, I soon learned that the organization also owed over $40,000 in unpaid back taxes to the IRS and the state Taxation and Revenue Department. I heard two versions of how the debt—which Gerry called an albatross around our neck—originated and accumulated, but it didn't matter now. The Feds and the state were threatening to foreclose on the organization and nobody was dealing with the real threat of complete and total shutdown.

Gerry was a good national Indian leader, but he was not an administrator. So, my first job as associate director was to team up with NIYC ally and retired accountant Ray Geotting (Caddo) to deal directly with the IRS and state revenue agents hovering over our office like vultures. In the process, I became NIYC's official accountant and Ray and I began formal negotiations with the IRS and the state. In the end, the negotiations were successful and we brought the total debt down to an amount that we could pay off. We created a new fund to pay this negotiated-down amount by radically rebudgeting the remaining balance of our Field Foundation grant. By December, we finally had the situation under control. It also helped that the Field Foundation had just renewed its critical funding that would support our advocacy work for calendar year 1975.

My second job as AD involved teaming up with Gerry and NIYC volunteer and UNM graduate student Al Henderson in early September to complete our application to the Labor Department to become a designated prime sponsor to administer a large grant under the new CETA program to serve all off-reservation Indians in New Mexico. After our application was approved, we flew to Oklahoma City to meet with our regional program director, who briefed us on the programmatic and financial responsibilities of prime sponsorship. She then told us to submit a Request for Proposal package to the Department of Labor. Facing a challenging deadline, we returned to Albuquerque and worked long nights at the office to expeditiously complete and submit the Request for Proposal package in a timely manner. After our grant proposal and budget were approved, we rented additional office space next door and hired the initial staff needed to start up the statewide program. We also established field offices in Gallup, Farmington, and Santa Fe.

Then, in December, the new NIYC CETA program director and I flew to Stillwater, Oklahoma to meet with CETA's national Indian program director Alexander "Sandy" MacNabb (Micmac) who conducted a two-day orientation session for CETA Indian program prime sponsors and grantees in the Greater Southwest region.

In late August, Sandy and Idaho Inter-Tribal Policy Board program developer Carole Wright (Western Shoshone) developed NIYC-specific guidelines that would allow our organization to operate an Indian investigative journalism training project as part of our CETA program. It was the first and only such training project in the country. Sandy had worked for several years on the Navajo reservation and was familiar with the lack of employment opportunities for the Navajo people. Carole was one of ten editors of Indian newspapers invited to form the American Indian Press Association (AIPA). She was also editor of Idaho's *Native Gem* and an investigative journalist in Indian Country.

By September, AIPA news director Richard LaCourse (Yakima) had relocated from Washington, DC to Albuquerque, where he now shared offices with us. Richard was a news journalist with considerable experience and his presence turned out to be a real advantage to NIYC's Investigative Journalism Training (IJT) Project. From our offices, Richard coordinated the fifth annual AIPA convention at the Institute of American Indian Arts in Santa Fe. Gerry and I went to that November convention and met with Richard and Sandy to discuss the mechanics of setting up the NIYC-IJT Project. We later had a private meeting with Sandy in Stillwater—a follow-up to the Santa Fe meeting—and, as a result, the NIYC CETA IJT Project was officially scheduled to start in February 1975.

As we closed out 1974, NIYC was in good shape. The $40,000 back tax debt was no longer a problem and we would pay our taxes on time going forward. In four months, we went from operating one office to operating five offices (including the CETA program headquarters in Albuquerque) and our staff went from three and a half persons (I was technically on half-time) to fifteen and a half persons. Our overall budget was now in the neighborhood of $400,000 and growing. With our basic resource base stabilized and secured for the long haul, Gerry wanted NIYC to become more of a "Nader's Raiders" kind of organization with strong research and legal capabilities. I remember him telling me, "Before, whenever anything came up, all we could do was call a press conference."

We worked toward his vision of NIYC as a major local, regional, and national powerhouse in Indian affairs. For organizational growth and development to occur at this ambitious scale, we needed to fundraise like hell. Gerry, myself, and our new CETA program director Tom Heidlebaugh (a white guy; Gerry's choice as program director, not mine) formed a fundraising team—primarily us three. Much of what I did at NIYC was co-administration, program development, and fundraising, with some organizing on the side. It was full-time work (though I was paid part-time). Since I was still going to school full-time, I worked afternoons, evenings, and weekends.

———

JoAllan generally supported my full-time work effort. During the late summer and early fall, she was harassed and intimidated by the FBI, which kept questioning her about my activities. They would question her at work. Then they tried questioning her at home. I was used to their tactics, but JoAllan wasn't. I had been under FBI and state police surveillance since at least 1972. Personally, I think they targeted JoAllan because she and I had worked together as an effective team, particularly during the summer of 1974, and they wanted to break us up by turning her into an informant.

Fortunately, we had our attorney Tom Luebben from the Albuquerque-based Native American Legal Defense and Education Fund (NALDEF) with us when the Feds showed up at our apartment. In their presence, Tom advised JoAllan not to answer any of their questions. That did it. It was the last time she had a direct encounter with them—even though we knew that our apartment was probably still wiretapped, our phone was probably bugged, and we would likely still be followed to activist functions.

Tom was always there when we needed him in urgent matters. He was with us when we marched in militarized Gallup on March 31, 1973. He was with us again when we marched in over-armed and dangerous Farmington on May 11, 1974. Tom and fellow NALDEF staff attorney Richard Young had advised us—Kiva Club and IAE—during the many intense strategy meetings at the UNM Native American Studies Center (NASC) in response to the crisis situations in Gallup and Wounded Knee. NALDEF executive director John Belindo (Navajo-Kiowa) also marched with us in exploitive Gallup on March 31, 1973 and again in racist Farmington on May 11, 1974. Later, John gave us a voice on his new weekly thirty-minute interview program, *First Americans,* on KOAT-TV. Another person I trusted with my life in those times was Junella Haynes of NASC, who first introduced me to Tom, Richard, and John of NALDEF. Always helpful, always available, day or night, Junella was the best.

In late 1974, NALDEF ran out of money and was forced to close its doors. Gerry and I then met with Tom and offered him a position as NIYC's director of litigation. Over coffee and toast at Mannie's the next morning, he accepted our generous offer (litigation program directorship, $500 a month, and a legal secretary) and promptly brought over five major cases he had been working on at NALDEF. We quickly hired a temporary legal secretary through our CETA program. Then, Gerry, Tom, and I immediately began aggressive fundraising to support the operation and planned expansion of our new litigation program.

I also raised additional general support funds from Tom Campbell, who had moved from Santa Fe to Galisteo, where he formed a foundation called Simpatico that held regional benefit concerts in the Southwest and the West Coast to fundraise for Indian and environmental movements. His group also funded Hopi and Chumash traditionalists in Arizona and California.

During this time, we also demonstrated at the Red Rock State Park ground-breaking ceremony, where we had a brief confrontation with Governor Bruce King and the state police. Using our Santa Fe CETA field office as a base, we shamelessly lobbied against proposed state funding for the Gallup Ceremonial. In perfect lock-step, we worked with CNL and newly-elected Navajo tribal councilman Fred Johnson on a coordinated follow-up to the civil rights hearings and ongoing investigation by the Civil Rights Commission and Justice Department. We deliberately staffed our Farmington CETA field office with CNL organizers like Dick Charley and Esther Keeswood, who continued to raise hell. In Albuquerque, we took the lead in organizing an urban Indian coalition that soon founded and directed the first Albuquerque Urban Indian Center (AUIC) on North Second. Gerry and I represented NIYC on the new AUIC board of directors.

While all this was going on, some Chicano allies asked me to go to Red China with them for a month. I politely declined since I was stretched in ten different directions. Besides, I didn't even have a passport.

Finally, on New Year's Eve, Glen Paquin and his wife Evelyn invited JoAllan and I for a quiet evening of cocktails and dancing at the Pow Wow Club to ring in the New Year.

———

1975 brought new challenges. And new resolve to meet the challenges.

After making up one incomplete from the fall semester, I wisely signed up for only twelve hours for the spring semester and I scheduled my classes for the morning so that I could continue to work on weekday afternoons and evenings. Now that I had a steady job, I qualified for a VA home loan, so JoAllan and I got a nice three-bedroom adobe house with a big backyard on Valencia NE. Gerry lived nearby, so we invited him over a lot for dinner or a barbeque on the front lawn. The three of us went out to places like Gerry's favorite French restaurant south of the university or to the Lobo Theater on Friday nights to watch Groucho Marx films and other old Hollywood classics. Life was good, work was good, and school for me was going pretty good too.

In late February, JoAllan and I flew to Oklahoma City for a meeting of the NEA First American Task Force. The two-day meeting included a site visit to the Cheyenne-Arapaho Institute of the Southern Plains in Hammon. I went on this trip because NIYC had helped establish the Indian-controlled community school. Then, in April, we flew to Washington, DC for a task force follow-up meeting. After the two-day meeting, task force member Billie Masters (Cherokee) gave me a beautiful necklace that she had made. Later that month, JoAllan and I found out our first child was due to be born in January 1976.

After my successful completion (as in no incompletes) of the spring semester in mid-May, I told JoAllan and Gerry that I was not going back to school for a while and would continue to work full-time for NIYC. It was the right thing to do. Furthermore, being paid full-time for full-time work would definitely help with new home and family expenses. I was also constantly asked to do public speaking for my job, which involved out-of-town travel—and the speaking and traveling commitments would only increase.

During the last eight and a half months, NIYC had grown dramatically. We now had a multi-building complex on the corner of Hermosa and Copper in Albuquerque's Nob Hill District. The complex consisted of fifteen offices, two reception areas, and a conference room where we held weekly staff directors meetings. We had a full-time staff of seventeen Indians and three non-Indians. The non-Indians were Tom Heidlebaugh, Tom Luebben, and Steve Nickeson. Steve was a former national investigative reporter for the *Race Relations Reporter* in Nashville and one of the co-directors of our CETA Investigative Journalism Training Project. The other co-director was Carole Wright, who had edited Indian newspapers in Nevada, Colorado, and Idaho. In addition to directing AIPA's national Indian news service, Richard LaCourse assisted Steve and Carole in providing investigative research and writing skills training to twenty-five Indian college students, mostly from the University of New Mexico. Several staff members from the American Indian Law Center assisted the IJTP co-directors in teaching students how to conduct legal and legislative research and analysis.

We were creative and innovative with our CETA program in other areas aside from the traditional employment and training services. Our diversified CETA operation offered a unique, culture-based ex-offender component as well as an outstanding technical assistance unit specializing in arts and crafts cooperative development. The CETA field offices in Gallup, Farmington, and Santa Fe added six more to our growing staff (now at twenty-six).

Although NIYC did not hold its annual organizational meeting in 1974, we held a group meeting on the Mescalero Apache reservation in August. Longtime NIYC member Bernard Second (Mescalero Apache) hosted the two-day meeting at his sacred mountain camp. On the second day, board elections were held and nine new and old board members were elected or re-elected. Among the new board members were Bernard, Herbert Blatchford, Sr., Al Henderson, and James Nez. Herb was also selected to serve as board vice president. I had gone to great lengths to make sure that Herb rejoined our group. After he left Gallup in 1973, he lived and worked in Phoenix. Although I had known him since 1970, I never had the opportunity to work with him. Now, I wanted to make sure that he moved to Albuquerque so we could finally work together. When he agreed to move and work at NIYC, I created a special job position for him through our CETA program. He would serve as our senior adviser since he had co-founded and directed NIYC in Gallup in the early and mid-sixties. Herb was one of my heroes in the national Red Power movement.

Gerry was another one of my movement heroes, and working with him was a dream come true. Working at NIYC on important issues was a dream job, but having the special honor and unique privilege of working with legends like Gerry and Herb made me feel like I was part of something great—something historic. It was like destiny. Yes, working for a Greater Indian America!

We had a board meeting in Albuquerque in early October and that's when Herb made his move from Phoenix. He arrived around the same time that Richard LaCourse left. AIPA had run out of operating funds and, like NALDEF, was forced to close. Although we were all sad to see Richard go, he was going back home to Toppenish, Washington to edit his tribal newspaper, the *Yakima Nation Review*. After I got Herb set up, we went to Fat Humphrey's for lunch and talked about the challenges of survival fundraising over iced tea and hoagies.

We had the Field Foundation and the Labor Department-funded CETA program. They were pretty reliable as funders. As long as we did good work consistently, they would continue to fund us. Gerry was also working with fundraising consultants Elizabeth Broder and Ben Peterson in New York on a national direct mail campaign. So far, though, they were netting more money than we were. Despite our concentrated fundraising efforts, the litigation program was still underfunded, but cost-effective as long as none of our cases went to a full-blown trial that could get expensive. Fortunately, they were strong cases with a number of plaintiffs' motions for summary judgments filed and pending decisions before the various courts. I was also still working with Tom Campbell of Simpatico. In the spring and fall, we had a series of very successful (and profitable) benefit concerts in Flagstaff and Santa Fe, bringing in top performers like Buffy Sainte-Marie (Cree), Jackson Browne, Nitty Gritty Dirt Band, Willie Nelson, Michael Martin Murphey, and Linda Ronstadt. We also manned our own food stands in Santa Fe, where we made and sold red and green chile stew and fry bread to the throngs of hungry concertgoers.

Gerry and I also met with Santa Fe author Stan Steiner who told us that there were over a hundred millionaires in the City Different and suggested that we approach them for big money. Later Stan helped us open a few doors and we got five thousand here and five thousand there, but nothing large and certainly no dedicated wills or legacies. I guess we just weren't cut out for that kind of high-society fundraising. As radical militants, we would have been more comfortable holding up trading posts.

Gerry was also working with Don Devereux and Steve Goldin of the Santa Fe-based Southwestern Institute to raise funds from the Stern Fund and the Community Trust Fund of New York to conduct power structure research on who owned and controlled San Juan County. If the proposed San Juan County Research Project was funded, NIYC would be the lead organization and would employ Steve Nickeson, Charlie Cambridge, and three graduates of our Investigative Journalism Training Project as guerilla researchers. Our project partners would be Southwestern Institute, Southwest Research and Information Center, and *Seers Catalogue* (a local weekly alternative newspaper with an emphasis on investigative reporting). They would hire their own researchers out of their share of the joint project funds.

Nodding his head, Herb acknowledged our present fundraising efforts and then recommended we also go directly to the major funders with both general support and project-specific proposals. We should also go as soon as possible since they generally operate on a calendar year funding cycle. Potential funders included the foundations, churches, and individual philanthropists. Herb told us to prepare thoroughly and bring the A-Team.

Within a month, Gerry, myself, Herb, and Tom Luebben were in the air, flying on the red-eye special to New York City for a ten-day fundraising mission. Elizabeth Broder and Ben Peterson met us at the airport and drove us to their apartment in Manhattan, where we stayed before moving on to Gerry's friend, filmmaker Lionel Rogosin, who introduced us to Black Power and Pan-African revolutionary Stokely Carmichael (Kwame Ture). Stokely was another one of my heroes and I was thrilled to meet him for the first time. He spoke at UNM in 1973 and JoAllan tape-recorded his speech, which I later played over and over again. The fundraising trip to New York was a tremendous success and we had Herb Blatchford to thank for it. I honestly believe that we could not have done as well as we did without him. It was my first time in the Big Apple and my introduction to the world of big-time fundraising.

Herb later helped us develop an organizational brochure and write an annual report of our activities for NIYC Year 1975. Expertly formatted and produced by Carole, the first-ever group brochure and annual report were designed to project our national profile and current statement of work to the funders and general public.

———

However, the bordertown work was unceasing.

In January, we continued to campaign against the Gallup Ceremonial and the Red Rock State Park but it was an uphill battle. We had asked the Navajo Tribe to deny access for the proposed extension of city utilities across tribal lands to the state park site, but it did not. Somebody must have gotten to the tribal chairman, Peter MacDonald, who had previously supported local Navajo opposition to the encroaching development project. After the tribe granted right-of-way access to the City of Gallup, there was no way to stop the completion of the state park, which was scheduled to host the Ceremonial in August. All we could do was encourage an Indian boycott of the annual event.

In February, Emmett Garcia called me out of the blue and requested a meeting in Albuquerque. The last time I saw Emmett was in July 1974 at the McKinley Area Council of Governments (MACOG) office in Gallup, where I had gone to see my old friend Elizabeth Kayate (Laguna Pueblo) about the precise role of the Joint Powers Commission, which was a member of MACOG. Elizabeth was now a planner at the regional agency. Garcia was meeting with MACOG director Jeff Meyer, who used to work with Emmett when he was mayor and chairman of the Gallup Interagency Alcoholism Coordinating Committee. After his meeting with Jeff and my meeting with Elizabeth, we met in the lobby on our way out. I couldn't think of anything nice to say—so I just told him that we weren't through with him yet. From his look of shock, I didn't think he'd ever want to see me again.

Seven months later, he called to say he wanted to pass on some confidential information on the mysterious Southwest Indian Foundation in Gallup, which was run by Franciscan Father Dunstan Schmidlin and was soliciting funds nationwide on behalf of the "poor Indians." Emmett claimed these funds were often used against him when he was mayor. He actually wanted me to meet with a man who was supposedly writing a book about Emmett Garcia and his political enemies in Gallup in the early seventies. His chief political enemies at the time were Rudy Carrillo and Pete Maldonado of the Zia Urban Renewal Project on Gallup's North Side. I already knew that. In a rather bizarre conspiracy theory, however, Emmett told me that Rudy, Pete, former Gallup mayor Eddie Munoz, then-North Side councilmen Sam Ray and Melcor Tafoya, and certain members of the Gallup Catholic Indian Center (not to be confused with the Gallup Indian Community Center) used Larry Casuse to work against him in late 1972 and early 1973.

I told him that IAE was not used by anybody and that we first opposed him after he tried to take control of the Gallup Indian Community Center in early 1972. I also told him that I thought the alleged author (who was sitting with us in a rented room at the Four Seasons Hotel) was really a private investigator hired to pick my brain about his political enemies. They didn't dispute my statement. The day after our meeting, Junella Haynes called to say that an author was hanging around the Native American Studies Center and asking questions. I then told her about my encounter with him and Emmett Garcia the day before—it was all a little strange, but we had important work to do.

In March, Al Henderson, Elva Benson (who had transferred from Yale to UNM), and the Kiva Club organized the second annual Larry Casuse Memorial at the Gallup Indian Community Center. In August, we issued a national call for a boycott of the 53rd Gallup Ceremonial. The boycott was effective and the state-funded Ceremonial lost thousands of dollars of taxpayer money.

———

In December, I met with Rena Harrison (Navajo), whose husband Franklin was now facing the death penalty for allegedly committing a crime against a non-Indian in Gallup. She strongly felt that Franklin was yet another Navajo victim of the white man's double standard of justice. Non-Indians can literally get away with murdering Indians but Indians face the gas chamber when they allegedly commit crimes against non-Indians. Rena also believed that her husband was wrongfully convicted and that he deserved a retrial. I told her that I would speak to Jim Toulouse and see if we could arrange a meeting. I was then contacted by Larry Casuse's mother, Lillian, about suing the Gallup police department in connection with the death of her son. The statute of limitations for filing a civil damage suit was three years. I also told Lillian that I would talk to

Mr. Toulouse and see if we could arrange a meeting with her. I then spoke to Jim regarding both matters and he said that we could meet separately with Rena and Lillian in Albuquerque or Gallup in early 1976 and then I separately got back in touch with the two women about Jim's offer.

In February, the legal trials of the CNL leadership were held in Farmington. Lorenzo LeValdo, Wilbert Tsosie, and I were found guilty by the city judge (who used to be a Farmington police officer and a San Juan County Sheriff) for causing the June 8, 1974 Main Street Riot. Wilbert and I appealed our wrongful convictions to the state district court in Aztec. However, the district court judge (who had helped incite the Sheriff's Posse Parade riot with his light sentencing of the three white teenage killers of the three Navajo men) dismissed our appeal in June. It was a conspiracy. In July, the US Civil Rights Commission issued the famous Farmington Report that found the "racist and sick" bordertown guilty as charged. Of course, we were right all along.

That same month, Al Henderson and I worked with attorney Tim Meehan of the San Juan County Economic Opportunity Council to investigate the suspicious circumstances surrounding the recent deaths of two Navajo men in the Farmington city jail. Our investigation culminated in a public demonstration outside the Farmington police station by members of the CNL and the surviving families of the deceased Navajo men. We also met with the police chief and the department's community relations officer. We later met with the federal Justice Department, which launched its own investigation into the criminal conditions at the jail, unrestrained police brutality, and a disturbing pattern of gross violations of prisoners' civil rights based on race. The department was also investigating two possible violations of the 1965 Voting Rights Act in San Juan County. Its civil rights division was exploring the possibility of suing the Selma of the Southwest for massive employment discrimination based on findings and recommendations of the recently released Farmington Report. Our meeting with the Justice Department on the Farmington and San Juan County legal matters took place in Jim Toulouse's office. But Jim's motto was: "Why meet about doing it? Just do it!" The Toulouse law firm filed two wrongful death lawsuits against the City of Farmington in the US District Court in Albuquerque on behalf of the families of the Navajo men who died as a result of untreated medical conditions in the city jail. December ended with us on the offensive and in a position of strength.

At its October meeting, the NIYC board also authorized the litigation program to file a lawsuit against US Secretary of Interior Thomas Kleppe and other Interior Department and BIA defendants to halt the continued violation of Indian student rights at the Intermountain Boarding School in Brigham City, Utah. The board decision was made after hearing a deeply moving presentation by longtime NIYC member and field representative Emma Delgarito (Navajo) on behalf of the students whose rights were violated. The NIYC litigation program now had six major legal cases. We had also just filed a pair of class action employment discrimination complaints with the federal Equal Employment Opportunity Commission (EEOC) against the State of New Mexico and the University of New Mexico (I worked with recent UNM graduate Glen Paquin on the latter complaint). We were also preparing to file similar complaints with the EEOC against the City of Farmington and the City of Albuquerque.

The litigation program also hosted a national meeting of Indian attorneys whose tribal clients wished to pursue treaty-based possessory land claims cases. Some of the clients included treaty tribes, such as the Oglala Sioux and Western Shoshone nations. We also discussed the related subject of international law at the two-day meeting co-sponsored by NIYC and the Institute for the Development of Indian Law.

In September, I met with Yakima fishing rights activist Sid Mills of the Survival of American Indians Association (SAIA) about a national caravan from Seattle to Washington, DC that his group was organizing to protest the American Bicentennial in 1976. The cross-country caravan would be similar to the 1972 Trail of Broken

Treaties caravan (the northern route started in Seattle under SAIA's leadership). Sid, a Trail of Broken Treaties and Wounded Knee veteran, explained that the 1976 caravan would be the Trail of Self-Determination and would come through Albuquerque on the way to the nation's capital. I told him we would support the caravan and organize a regional rally in Albuquerque when they came through. SAIA and NIYC had worked together on Fish-Ins in the Northwest in the sixties. Herb Blatchford, the first NIYC executive director, was a major leader in the regional and national Indian fishing rights protests and SAIA's first executive director, Hank Adams (Assiniboine Sioux), was an early NIYC board member. As part of the second wave of NIYC Red Power activists, I looked forward to working with Sid and our sister organization in 1976.

———

The first month of the new year began with great joy and deep sadness. JoAllan gave birth to a beautiful baby boy, who we named John Kayah. I always liked the name Kayah. Fred Johnson, the brave CNL leader and brilliant Shiprock councilman, also named his first son Kayah. His second son, Fred Jr., was born one month before John K. On January 3, Fred Sr. and I talked about fatherhood during a break at a meeting at the Shiprock chapterhouse. Three days later, he was killed in a mysterious small airplane crash near Grants. He had often visited our Albuquerque headquarters and, on his last visit, called our work with the New Mexico Indian prison inmates and paroled ex-offenders "a dream come true." We served as the organizational sponsor of the Native American Brotherhood at the state penitentiary and our CETA ex-offender component was now a full program in the organization.

Organizationally, we continued to expand. In addition to the statewide ex-offender program, we now had a citywide youth recreation program directed by Ramona Wilgus. The youth recreation center was located in a large building on Second and Mountain. The CETA manpower program continued to grow and develop. Our litigation program also added a new attorney, Marcia Wilson, who used to work with DNA People's Legal Services. First-year law school student Susan Tomita (Hawaiian-Alaskan Native) also interned with us in the summer of 1976. Law school graduate George Harrison began externing with us in the winter. By then, we had won two major cases and had filed two more lawsuits. We had also filed a class action employment discrimination complaint against the City of Albuquerque. And it appeared to be just a matter of time before we would file a similar complaint with the EEOC against the City of Farmington.

After a two-year hiatus, we began republishing our national newspaper, *Americans Before Columbus,* co-edited by former IJTP co-director Carole Wright and IJTP graduate Manuel Pino (Acoma Pueblo). Carole and Manny also started a research and publications program. Recent UNM graduate Louise Four Horns operated and maintained our new resource library and reading room.

Former IJTP co-director Steve Nickeson started the jointly funded San Juan County Research Project in Albuquerque and Farmington. Former IAE summer work project employee Robert Tohe (Navajo) headed our new electronic media advocacy project. He also succeeded John Belindo as host of *First Americans.* Circle Films, a national Indian film production company directed by Ron Sarracino (Laguna Pueblo), soon came into our fold. In addition, we opened a joint NIYC-CNL field office in Fred Johnson's former office at the Shiprock chapterhouse that was directed by Esther Keeswood. We also rented a field organizing and lobbying office at the DNA People's Legal Services headquarters in Window Rock. We used the WR field office when the Navajo tribal council was in session or whenever there was a need to raise hell in the tribal capital.

We still had functioning NIYC chapters or projects in Arizona, Utah, Oklahoma, Wisconsin, and North Carolina, and Gerry was still doing his cutting-edge international work with Indians in Mexico and Canada. The new NIYC board was active and engaged, meeting in Boulder in the spring and Albuquerque in the fall. We also had a staff retreat in the Sangre De Cristo Mountains. Herb led the two-day retreat. We now had a staff of fifty people and our over-all budget was more than half a million dollars. As CEOs, Gerry and I were getting overwhelmed. It was very difficult to administer and organize at the same time. So, we appointed Carole as our administrative officer and accountant Ken Tsosie (Navajo) as our financial officer to help us run the organization more efficiently. The Big Five—Gerry, myself, Carole, Ken, and Herb—formed an in-house leadership council to provide effective management direction to the greatly expanded scope of work.

———

With the leadership council system in place, I became more of a family man and I loved it. On Presidents' Day weekend, John Kayah and I stayed home and bonded while JoAllan went to DC for her NEA First American Task Force meeting. That's when I discovered that he liked Godfather's Pizza with green chiles. It was all I could do to keep up with the little tiger. In late May and early June, the three of us spent a relaxing nine-day vacation in Phoenix and Los Angeles. We visited Disneyland, Santa Monica Beach, and, of course, Moby's Dock overlooking the beautiful Pacific Ocean at sunset. We also visited some of JoAllan's friends in LA and Lancaster (where she taught school in 1969–70). In July, JoAllan and Kayah spent the month in Tempe and I flew down every weekend to visit them. JoAllan was attending summer school at Arizona State University for her master's degree, which she received at the end of the month. We celebrated at a funky greasy spoon diner in Benson off I-10 on the way back to Albuquerque. In late December and early January, we returned to balmy southern Arizona and vacationed poolside under the tall palm trees in Tempe and Tucson. Family life was very good.

Kayah was three months old and seated intently in his stroller when the Trail of Self-Determination came to town. JoAllan and I took turns pushing his stroller as we joined the 250 anti-Bicentennial protestors who marched from UNM, down Central, to the Albuquerque Civic Plaza, where a major regional rally was held to support the cross-country caravan on its way to the nation's capital.

NIYC and the Kiva Club co-sponsored the two-mile march and support rally.

The caravan went on to Washington, DC where Native delegates delivered a historic manifesto on Indian sovereignty and treaty rights. On their way back, some of the caravan delegates and supporters dropped by the office to brief us on their meetings with government officials and future plans regarding follow-up. I also met with caravan participant Roberto Maestas of the Seattle-based El Centro De La Raza, who said that he and fellow trail participant and journalist Bruce Johansen were going to write a book on the continuing Indian Wars and wanted me to help them with the section on the Southwest. I agreed and then directed them to our Shiprock field office, which had just mounted an impressive and effective campaign aimed at shutting down the controversial Turquoise Bar west of Farmington. I also contacted Esther to set up a special tour of the Four Corners area for the two authors.

———

Our bordertown work in 1976 was characterized by ups and downs. Herb and I met with New Mexico Governor Jerry Apodaca about defunding the waste of state money called the Ceremonial. When he failed to take proper executive action, NIYC issued a national call for a boycott of the 54th Gallup Ceremonial at the Red Rock State Park. Due in large part to the public boycott, the state-subsidized Ceremonial Association took it in the shorts—the poorly attended four-day event lost thousands of dollars of taxpayer money for the second straight year. After several meetings in Gallup and Albuquerque, Jim Toulouse agreed to represent Franklin Harrison in his petition for a retrial. We also met with Lillian Casuse in Gallup. The suits arising out of the wrongful deaths of the two Navajo men in the Farmington city jail in 1975 were dismissed in favor of the defendants who still looked guilty. In our eyes, the city's criminal negligence involved in the men's deaths was effectively legalized by the arbitrary dismissals. We hoped the Justice Department would have something to say about that in its investigation of the jail.

1977 was a mixed bag. Because of our continued successful fundraising, we now had so much money that Gerry and I decided to give ourselves a modest raise. Up until now, we had paid ourselves only $8,000 a year each. We were obviously stuck in 1974. Even the organization's program directors and assistant directors were making more money than we were. That included litigation program director Tom Luebben, who was no longer working for $500 a month. So, Gerry and I did a little bit of fancy dancing on the books and gave ourselves a $2,000-a-year raise each. Without telling JoAllan, I immediately cashed my two grand and treated my family to a surprise nine-day vacation to California. The three of us went to Fisherman's Wharf and Chinatown in San Francisco, Magic Mountain, and Wally World in Los Angeles, and the world-famous zoo and Sea World in San Diego. While in San Diego, I offered to buy JoAllan a diamond ring since I couldn't afford to buy her a wedding ring when we got married in the summer of 1974.

OOPS! It was the oops heard around the world. I didn't tell her where or how I got the extra money! "But honey, it was supposed to be a surprise—all of it." No good. A week later, she filed for divorce and I was sleeping at the office.

One good thing about those thick environmental impact statements I read during the day was that they made comfortable pillows at night. After two months of Chinese takeout and sleeping on the floor, I finally got a nice luxury townhouse apartment on Graceland SE. Two months later, I got a brand-new car—a 1977 orange Ford Pinto I named Bessie. Me and Bessie became best buds.

With my personal and family life down the tubes, I just threw myself into my work. Gerry also picked a good time to go to Mexico for six weeks because that made me acting director on a twenty-four seven basis for the next month and a half. And there was plenty to direct and crises to manage. The organization now had over fifty full-time employees and a budget of at least $1.5 million. We had money coming in from foundations, churches, individual philanthropists, direct mail donors, governmental agencies (federal, state, and city), the Navajo Tribe, and anonymous folks who just left bags of cash on our doorstep at night. The more money we had, the more work we could do, so our staffing grew, our programs grew, our projects grew (except for the San Juan County Research Project which ended), our components grew, and we established a central accounting department to handle it all. We also added a new project, the Albuquerque-Bernalillo County Native American Voter Registration and Education Project. I chaired the project's steering committee and we selected Louise Four Horns (who had a political science degree from UNM) to direct the project.

We also helped establish the Albuquerque Native American Affirmative Action Council to implement the negotiated conciliation agreement signed by NIYC and the City of Albuquerque that settled the class action employment discrimination complaint that we had filed against the city in 1976. The historic agreement was "the first of its kind in the country." In addition, we resurrected our Investigative Journalism Training Project. Carole directed the project (in addition to her other work duties) and Steve Nickeson served as a project consultant. Although we did not have a board meeting in 1977, we did have a two-day staff retreat in the Jemez Mountains and Herb started a weekly talking circle series.

We effectively campaigned against the state-funded Gallup Ceremonial, which lost thousands of taxpayer dollars for the third year in a row. Franklin Harrison got his retrial but it ended in a mistrial. Justice redenied. We presented strong testimony and solid documentation at a public hearing held by the New Mexico State Advisory Committee to the US Civil Rights Commission in Farmington on the current status of civil rights in the racist bordertown. Following the hearing, the committee issued a scathing report that sustained our indictment against the Selma of the Southwest. The Shiprock field office was also taking care of business in San Juan County. After a six-month NIYC-CNL campaign, the notorious Turquoise Bar had its liquor license suspended for six months and its non-Indian owner and operator was fined for numerous state liquor law violations. This citizen-pressured state action served as a model of exemplary grassroots organizing and community mobilization.

When I met with Sid Mills in 1975, he mentioned a growing anti-Indian backlash to a 1974 federal court decision that upheld Northwest Indian fishing rights that were protected by the 1854 Treaty of Medicine Creek. By 1977, the regional backlash had grown into a strong national campaign against Indian sovereignty and treaties led by the hateful and dangerous Interstate Congress for Equal Rights and Responsibilities (ICERR).

In January, Carole began a six-month investigative research study into the powerful white backlash movement and ICERR. In June, she wrote a summary report of her findings that was then published in our newspaper, *Americans Before Columbus*, and a special backlash edition of *Yakima Nation Review* (edited by Richard LaCourse). She also presented the findings of her report at the plenary session of the National Congress of American Indians' annual mid-year convention in Albuquerque. In December, she attended a national Indian strategy meeting in Phoenix to deal with the serious backlash threat.

On New Year's Eve, I picked Carole up and we went to Okie's for a couple pitchers of beer and boogied the night away to the jukebox music of the Bee Gees and others.

———

After the fireworks, it was back to work again.

In terms of fundraising, 1978 was even more successful than 1977. Gerry and I gave ourselves another modest raise, bringing our annual salaries to $12,000 each. The organization continued to expand its activities, staff, programs, projects, and components. We also added two more projects (paralegal training and environmental education) and rented two more office buildings (one of them was, ironically, located within the old Sunbell plant complex). We established the Native American Appropriate Technology Action Council to guide the development of our Navajo solar hogan demonstration project. Heading the council was Ross Smallcanyon (Navajo). We also held a two-day staff retreat in the Manzano Mountains.

In 1978, we filed two new lawsuits and hired two new attorneys, John Kelly and Roger Finzel, to replace Tom Luebben and Marcia Wilson, who were leaving. Although Tom went into private practice, he remained of counsel to NIYC. We also hired certified paralegal Aldine Farrier (Spokane) and recent UNM law school graduate Tonia Garcia (Nez Perce). Now a licensed attorney, George Harrison set up his own law office but continued to work with us.

In the spring, I hired Al Henderson to work with me after his wife, Elva Benson, recently passed away. They had a two-year-old daughter named Loya who was the same age as my son Kayah. Al and I worked together on a number of issues, including the CNL-led Aneth Oil Field takeover and The Longest Walk to protest anti-Indian congressional legislation. After Al left to become executive director of the Navajo tribal economic development division, I hired eighteen-year-old Harvard University student Winona LaDuke (Mississippi Chippewa) to work with me and Carole on Southwest Indian energy and environmental issues over the summer. During her stay, Winona hand made a beautiful shirt for me that I still have to this day.

From February to July, Manuel Pino, Arlene Luther (Navajo), Jene Hood (Yurok), and James Muneta (Navajo) of NIYC participated in The Longest Walk from Alcatraz Island to Washington, DC. In March, Herb and I spoke at a regional rally of the cross-country walk in Pueblo, Colorado. Al also attended the rally. In June, Carole and I worked with Navajo Longest Walk leaders Elvira Burnside (the coordinator of the Window Rock-based Diné Bi Professional Association), Shirley Martin, Joe Singer, and Norman Brown to form a reservation-wide coalition known as the Navajo Longest Walk Steering Committee (NLWSC). Carole also developed information resource materials for the new group.

Our organizational involvement with the group increased when the Navajo Tribe agreed to conditionally fund NLWSC to organize a delegation of youth and elders from Big Mountain, Aneth, and other traditional Navajo communities to travel to Washington, DC to participate in The Longest Walk events in the nation's capital in July. The condition was that the group had to have a fiscal sponsor for the administration of the tribal grant. Gerry and I worked with Bobby George, an executive staff assistant to Navajo Tribal Chairman Peter MacDonald, to develop a financial arrangement whereby NIYC would serve as fiscal sponsor for NLWSC's expenditure and accounting responsibility for the $15,000 grant (which was largely secured by Shirley, the steering committee coordinator). After several meetings in Albuquerque and Window Rock, the arrangement was worked out. The Navajo Longest Walk delegation later stopped by the office on their way to DC.

In the spring, Gerry and I also worked with Daniel Deschiney, another executive staff assistant to Navajo Tribal Chairman MacDonald, to help establish the first Native American Treaty Rights Organization (NATRO) conference in Window Rock. NATRO was founded by the Navajo Tribe to fight the metastasizing white backlash movement. The new umbrella group consisted of the Navajo Tribe, NIYC, AIM, International Indian Treaty Council, National Congress of American Indians, National Tribal Chairmen Association, Americans for Indian Opportunity, National Indian Brotherhood of Canada, Alaska Federation of Natives, and the Hawaiian Coalition of Natives. Tonia Garcia also developed legal education materials for the historic conference. Gerry spoke at the plenary session of the conference and Carole and I co-facilitated workshops on advocacy journalism and economic development.

I continued to serve as chairman of the Albuquerque-Bernalillo County Native American Voter Registration and Education Project Steering Committee. I also continued to serve on the National Council of Churches Energy Study Panel that I was appointed to in 1977 after being nominated by Reverend Jim West (Southern Cheyenne).

In the summer, I was appointed to the City of Albuquerque-Bernalillo County Air Quality Control Board and the New Mexico State Advisory Committee to the US Civil Rights Commission.

Gerry and John Dulles II were also lobbying to get me appointed to the new Regional Advisory Committee to the US Civil Rights Commission. Gerry and Chicano political activist Willie Velasquez were lobbying to get me appointed to the board of directors of the Southwest Voter Registration and Education Project, which was funding Indian voter registration and education projects in Albuquerque and Phoenix.

That summer, Roberto Maestas and Bruce Johansen asked me to write the introduction to their upcoming book *Wasichu: The Continuing Indian Wars.*

———

On August 1, 1978, I resigned as Associate Director of the National Indian Youth Council. This was partly to serve as interim project director of the NIYC's new New Mexico Indian Environmental Education Project that had received funding but hadn't started up. The start-up date for the project was September 1.

First, a word about the Indian environmental education project.

Figuring that we needed more Esther Keeswoods in the field, Herb Blatchford and I took the lead in the development of the then-proposed New Mexico Indian Environmental Education Project in early January. Based on Herb's excellent concept paper on the critical need for Native environmental education, we formed a fundraising team with paralegal Aldine Farrier (who came from the uranium-contaminated Spokane reservation in Washington) and Arlene Luther (who had a nursing background in environmental health) to mobilize necessary financial resources for the project. We team-wrote and submitted a proposal for $80,000 to carry out the statewide project. The project was later approved and we received full, renewable funding for the first year.

As interim project director, I recruited and hired investigative journalism training project graduate Lisa Chavez (San Felipe Pueblo) as the permanent director for the statewide project.

As project director, Lisa then hired the rest of the staff and consultants. I had agreed with Lisa to stay on as a consultant to assist her with the project's development.

From September to December, I mostly worked with project librarian Maurice Thompson (Navajo) on the development of the Environmental Resource Library. The library largely consisted of subject matter files, periodicals, documents, maps, and other resource materials that were loaned to the project by Elouise Chicharello (Navajo) of the UNM Native American Studies Center's American Indian History Project, Winona LaDuke, and myself. We had loaned our prized energy, environmental, and water files to be used for community education and organizing in Indian Country.

After I resigned as NIYC Associate Director, I met with Winona who had primarily worked with me and Carole since June. We both felt close to Winona and considered her our movement daughter. She stayed at our house for the first part of the summer before getting an apartment of her own. She had just returned from Cuba (the country, not the sleepy little village in Sandoval County) when she learned of my resignation. When we met on the lawn across from the NIYC headquarters in mid-August, she said she supported me and was going to skip her fall semester at Harvard so she could work with Lisa, me, and the new staff and consultants at the environmental education project office. Her personal sacrifice and deep commitment to the continuing work meant a lot to me since I was the one who hired her to work with us at NIYC. After our meeting, my heart soared like an eagle.

Following my resignation from NIYC, the position of associate director was eliminated and Gerry hired Cheryl Mann (Cheyenne River Sioux) to assist him in the administration of the organization.

I also resigned as chairman of the Albuquerque-Bernalillo County Native American Voter Registration and Education Project steering committee and from the City of Albuquerque-Bernalillo County Air Quality Control Board. However, I continued to serve as a member of the New Mexico State Advisory Committee to the US Civil Rights Commission and a member of the National

Council of Churches Energy Study Panel. My consultant work with the New Mexico Indian Environmental Education Project ended in December and I debriefed Lisa and Winona as part of the exit process.

There were, of course, other reasons why I resigned as NIYC Associate Director but that is another discussion.

PART II
RESOURCE WARS & CONTESTED TERRITORIES

CHAPTER 4

COAL AND WATER POLITICS
THREATEN NAVAJO SURVIVAL

Back in August of 1972, I met with Mitch Fowler in Gallup to compare notes on the proposed coal gasification complex development on the Navajo reservation. I had been following the proposed development scenario from a distance while Mitch had been educating and organizing people on the land. He was a co-founder and board vice president of the Chinle-based Committee to Save Black Mesa and had already brought a delegation of Navajos from the coal-rich lands of Black Mesa to the Burnham chapterhouse, where they informed local residents of the horrors of strip mining, which included forced relocation and massive environmental and cultural destruction. Mitch worked with Burnham chapter president, Eva Arthur, to facilitate the effective people-to-people community education presentation. This successfully planted the seeds of opposition in the Burnham chapter, which now resisted plans by a consortium of private companies to build two separate but related complexes of coal gasification plants, strip mines, and pipelines on lands the chapter members occupied and used.

I approached the coal mining and gasification issue by researching and writing about the adverse effects that the coal gas plants would have on Navajo tribal water rights in the San Juan River basin. Each coal gasification plant would use ten thousand acre-feet of water per year. Since there were plans to build a total of seven coal gas plants, this would draw a total of seventy thousand acre-feet of water from the San Juan River each year for twenty-five years—the planned operating life of the gasification plants. That was a lot of Navajo water. The Navajo Tribe had "prior and paramount" rights to the San Juan River basin water under the Indian reserved water rights doctrine known as the *Winters Doctrine,* which emerged from a US Supreme Court decision in the landmark case of *Henry Winters v. United States of America.* This case was doctrinally confirmed by another Supreme Court decision in another landmark case known as *Arizona v. California.* The Navajo Treaty of 1868 had established the priority date of tribal reservation water rights.

———

As early as 1947, the Bureau of Indian Affairs proposed the construction and operation of coal gasification (coal to gas) and coal liquefaction (coal to oil) plants in the Four Corners area of the rez. The proposed plan wasn't going to happen without large concessions of Navajo land, water, and coal. So, in 1953, the Indian bureau approved a permit for Utah Construction Company to explore and drill for mineable coal in the area between Nenahnezad and Burnham. Four years later, the Bureau approved a lease for Utah Construction and Mining Company (no longer just Utah Construction) to mine coal on twenty-four thousand acres (later expanded to thirty-one thousand acres overlying 1.1 billion tons of strip mineable coal) of Navajo grazing lands. In 1959, the Indian agency approved a permit for El Paso Natural Gas Company to explore and drill for mineable coal in the area between Burnham and Bisti. Nine years later, the agency approved a lease for El Paso and Consolidation Coal Company to mine coal on forty thousand acres of community grazing lands.

However, they needed water to mine the coal; so, that same year, 1968, the Department of Interior approved a water service contract for Utah to use forty-four thousand acre-feet of water per year from the San Juan River to convert (electrify, gasify, or liquefy) the coal in its mining lease. A year later, El Paso and Consolidation began to negotiate with Interior to approve a water service contract to use thirty thousand acre-feet of water per year from the Rio San Juan to convert (electrify, gasify, or liquefy) over eight hundred million tons of strippable coal they leased to mine.

Then, in 1971, El Paso and Consolidation (later known as CONPASO) filed an application with the Federal Power Commission (FPC) for a license to build three mine-mouth coal gasification plants on their coal mining lease at Burnham. That same year, the Texas Eastern Transmission Corporation and Pacific Lighting Corporation (later known as Western Gasification Company or WESCO) also filed an application with the FPC for a license to construct four mine-mouth coal gasification plants near Burnham. These plants would use most of the coal leased by Utah International, Inc. (formerly Utah Construction and Mining Company), which, like Consolidation, would do the mining. Utah International also planned to amend and transfer its water service contract to WESCO for its proposed gasification plants.

If constructed, the seven plants would be the nation's first and world's largest commercial coal gasification plants. In addition to the plants, mines, and pipelines, there were plans for a super man-camp and boomtown at Burnham to house fifty thousand people—mostly male outsiders. To accommodate the proposed megaprojects and new town, several hundred Burnham chapter residents would have to move out. In terms of benefits and costs, all of the synthetic natural gas (a great oxymoron) produced at the plants would be piped off the reservation to Texas and California. And all the significant adverse environmental and cultural impacts of the plants would stay on the reservation. Coal gasification on Navajo land was bad news. It was a frightful picture of planned genocide, ethnocide, and ecocide on a mass holocaust scale.

———

After our meeting in Gallup, Mitch continued to work with the Burnham chapter leadership on the coal gasification issue. I continued to research and write on the gasification water angle but was primarily working with IAE and the Kiva Club from September 1972 to May 1973.

As a result of his vanguard community education and organizing efforts, Mitch co-founded the Diné Coalition (DC), which was laser-focused on Navajo tribal government reform and the coal gasification issue. In late May 1973, I attended the first DC meeting at the Emerson family home in Hogback. Also attending the day-long meeting were Larry Emerson and his activist sisters Gloria and Elaine, Alice Luna of the Committee to Save Black Mesa, and June Toledo. Mitch and Alice reported on the committee's expanded work at Black Mesa and Burnham and the need to engage more Navajo environmental activists on a tribal reservation-wide level. "We need a coalition of strong Diné citizens and community activists," Mitch said, "a Diné Coalition to empower local communities and impact tribal government policies." Others spoke passionately and I was soon caught up in the spirit of the historic meeting. I volunteered to join the DC revolution and pledged to make coal gasification an IAE priority now that we had run Emmett Garcia out of town.

As IAE summer work projects coordinator, I prioritized coal gasification as our lead project. I hired Mitch as coal gasification project group leader and, together, we recruited and hired Iva Palucci, Elvira Burnside (formerly of the Committee to Save Black Mesa), Lillian Lewis (a Kiva Club member who was back home in Gallup for the summer), and Yvonne Crawford (daughter of Miriam Crawford of the Save Black Mesa Committee) as group workers. Also joining us in our gasification struggle were Elaine Emerson of Southwestern Indian Development (SID) and her brother Larry who wrote frontline articles for the American Indian Press Association News Service and *Americans Before Columbus*. Everybody worked long and hard for the next three months.

Before the summer was over, the Burnham chapter had overwhelmingly passed two resolutions opposing the proposed coal gasification and strip mining projects. We also demonstrated at the

Federal Building in Albuquerque, where the Bureau of Reclamation held a scoping meeting on the preparation of environmental impact statements (EIS) for the proposed gasification and mining projects. In addition, we testified at the public meeting and served notice on the Bureau of 'Wreck' that we would be in their face at every step of the required EIS process. That summer, we partnered with the Committee to Save Black Mesa to jointly support proposed national legislation to ban coal strip mining. The proposed legislation was a direct response to the new term and concept of "national sacrifice areas," which had leaked out of a draft study and report by the National Academy of Sciences on the reclamation potential of strip-mined lands in the arid Southwest. As the project ended, we worked with SID to participate in the first annual Navajo Nation Youth Conference held in Gallup and at Lake Assayi. On Labor Day weekend, Mitch and I set up a Diné Coalition coal gasification information booth at the Navajo Tribal Fair in Window Rock.

Mitch and I then drafted articles of incorporation and bylaws for the Diné Coalition and met with the corporate law firm of Duhigg and Cronin in Albuquerque for legal assistance in our application for IRS tax-exempt status as an educational non-profit organization. For incorporation purposes, Mitch asked me to serve as a registered agent for the Coalition (I had also served as a registered agent for IAE when that organization incorporated). Most groups needed to incorporate and obtain a tax-exempt status to get the necessary money to operate. So, after the Coalition was incorporated, we drafted a funding proposal for $50,000 and planned to finalize and submit it to the Ford Foundation as soon as we got our 501(c)(3) designation letter from the IRS.

We submitted our necessary paperwork, including an application for a tax-exempt status, to the IRS, but the letter of determination did not arrive within the normal processing period of six months. Six months and one day, still no word from the IRS, and, unfortunately, the Ford Foundation proposal deadline had passed. We had done everything right but some people—like Irwin R. Schyster—just don't play by their own rules. We could not wait for the unresponsive IRS or charitable philanthropy to assist us. As it were, Penny Hunter, Elvira Burnside, and I were too busy doing the necessary and important work of the Navajo Coal Gasification Project at UNM. Obviously, we could have used the money that would have made the work better and more effective—regardless, we were going to do the work anyway. Of course, we had to scrounge and sacrifice. I even sold blood (my blood!) to the needle-wielding vampires at the local plasma bank to help keep the bare-bones project going.

In late April 1974, Farmington happened and I was diverted again.

In July, the draft environmental impact statement was issued for the proposed CONPASO project. This was the first, but definitely not the last, massive EIS report that I would read. To properly review and comment on the technical document, I had to become familiar with the National Environmental Policy Act (NEPA) and its case law on Indian lands. As part of the critical document review process, I met with El Paso Natural Gas Company representative Charles Hunter at the San Juan County Economic Opportunity Council office. He was a little shaky, but I did manage to extract some rather useful water-related information about El Paso's application for an industrial water service contract for coal gas. I was still approaching the coal gasification issue from the water angle.

Then, in early September, NIYC happened and I was diverted again—but not as much.

In October, Gerry and I met with Western Gasification Company representative Dan Cook at the office. I had met with Dan before when the Diné Coalition truth squad crashed his spring party at UNM, which probably explained why he was so jumpy this time. The purpose of this meeting wasn't to beat him up or even get in a few good body blows (however well deserved). It was to get specific project information, particularly copies of a coal sales contract between Utah International, Inc. and WESCO, plus an amendatory water service contract that Utah International was planning to transfer to Texas Eastern Transmission Corporation and Pacific Lighting Corporation. He said that it was proprietary information. We reminded him that we could always file a Freedom of Information Act request (followed by a FOIA lawsuit if necessary) with the BIA and the Department of Interior since they have to officially act on (i.e., approve or deny) the contracts anyway. He started to hem-haw around. Finally, we told him that we can do this the easy way, or we can do it the hard way. Want to play hardball, Dan? It took a while, but we eventually got the information we had initially asked nicely for.

In November, I began participating in a yearlong New Mexico Humanities Council Land and Water Use lecture series at San Juan College in Farmington and the UNM branch in Gallup. As one of the invited panelists, I spoke on the Navajo coal gasification issue. I also met with newly elected Navajo tribal councilman Fred Johnson in Shiprock to help develop a legislative strategy that would effectively address the gasification issue in the council chambers in 1975. Fred and I also spoke at the first annual winter conference of the Coalition for Navajo Liberation at the Shiprock chapterhouse. We met with the new Shiprock Research Center director Harris Arthur, son of former Burnham chapter president Eva Arthur, who briefed us on the center's work assessing the projected social, economic, and environmental impacts of the proposed coal gasification development. Harris had previously told Fred that he wanted to hire me to work with him at the center. It was flattering but Harris never directly approached me. It didn't matter because there was plenty of work for everybody on the coal gas issue.

In December, I spoke on coal mining and gasification at the first public meeting of the new Navajo Tribal Environmental Protection Commission in Window Rock. My old fishing buddy from Farmington, Harold Tso, was the Commission staff director and his executive secretary was my favorite cousin, Caroline. Larry Emerson, whose thinking always aligned with mine, was one of the Commission's board members and officers. So, I took the unfettered opportunity to speak at length on the clear and present danger of coal gasification at Burnham and the northern Navajo Nation.

After the daylong meeting, Harold, Larry, and I huddled at a table in the cafeteria at the Window Rock Lodge and shared exciting ideas about the potential of the new Commission. The next day, I went over the hill and had a delicious Navajo taco at the Window Rock Motor Inn. After licking my plate clean, I got on the road and hitchhiked to Gallup where I caught the mid-morning train back to Albuquerque. The month and year ended, not with a bang, but with the issuance of the draft environmental impact statement for the proposed WESCO project. It arrived in the mail right before Christmas—a lump of coal in my Christmas stocking! I spent the joyous week between Christmas and New Year's analyzing the voluminous document. When I resurfaced a week later, I had to reintroduce myself to JoAllan (this was still 1974–75 and the proverbial honeymoon was not yet over—or maybe it was).

———

As I cleared my head from all this heavy document review, I noticed that the movement dynamics had changed. The Committee to Save Black Mesa was gone—out of money. The Diné Coalition was gone because it never got the money. Mitch was still around but no longer active in the coal gasification struggle—probably burned out and frustrated. Personally, I thought he was just ahead of his time. Anyway, through my efforts, NIYC had emerged as a major player in the coal gas struggle. Wilbert Tsosie of CNL and AIM's Larry Anderson had joined the coal gas struggle and became major organizational contributors. Harris Arthur's Shiprock Research Center was expanding and had recently hired Barbara West and Al Henderson as new staff members. Assisting Harris were his wife and 1974 ASU law school graduate Claudeen Bates Arthur and attorneys Richard Hughes and Robert Strumor of Shiprock DNA. Fred Johnson and the new Navajo tribal councilman, Lewis Etsitty from Nenahnezad, were leading the political opposition to coal gasification in Window Rock.

Coal gasification had become NIYC's leading issue and Gerry had designated me to lead the new organizational campaign. The organizing project ran from January 1975 to July 1978. A good blow-by-blow description of the three-and-a-half-year campaign is recorded in my NIYC coal gasification information packet series on file in my collection, the John Redhouse Papers, housed at the University of New Mexico Center for Southwest Research. No need to retell that old movement war story here. I continued to work on the coal mining and gasification issue after I left NIYC in 1978, first as a member of the American Indian Environmental Council and then as an individual. My post-1978 work on mining and gasifica-tion is also archived in my collection at the university.

———

I'm a conspiracy theory guy. Most of my friends, however, think I'm nuts. Whenever I give my take on something sinister, they always say, "John, it's not a conspiracy. You think everything's a conspiracy." I wasn't always a conspiracy theory nut. Before I became politically conscious, I was fairly normal. Then stuff happened, and I changed.

I grew up in Farmington in the fifties and sixties. It was a typical bordertown—racist as hell. There were the usual local rednecks, the ones whose eyes were genetically and generationally spaced closer together than most people. They didn't like Indians, but they liked our money. They would rather roll an Indian than kill one, although there were some whites who killed Indians. Then came the boom-ers, the white oilfield trash from Texas and Oklahoma, who were as dangerous as they looked. They hated Blacks but since there were very few Negroes and a whole lot of Indians in the new Energy Capital of the West, the local Indians became their niggers. Red niggers. The energy boom and its invasion of boomers was when Indian killing became a regular sport in Farmington. They would kill you just because you were an Indian. So, the bordertown bros like Fred Johnson, Sam Benally, Melvin Betsellie, Deland Pioche, me, and others who grew up in South Farmington and on the Peninsula grew up fighting during that particularly violent period. We had to fight back to survive. Or the local Hitler Youth would have beat us to death.

While we were fighting for our lives, we realized the supreme irony that most of the energy that made Farmington a boomtown came from the nearby Navajo, Jicarilla Apache, Southern Ute, and Ute Mountain Ute Indian reservations. Most of the water in the rivers flowing through our tribal lands was used for regional energy development that not only benefited the area boomers but large off-reservation, non-Indian populations in big cities like Albuquerque, El Paso, Phoenix, Tucson, Las Vegas, and Los Angeles. Oh my God, we were a colony, an exploited energy and water resource colony of the master race! Colonization was by design. The exploitation was part of a grand plan. We, in the border-town ghettoes, were fighting the sons of the colonizers and exploiters who had set up shop and were running their resource raids out of Farmington. We, the Indigenous people of this land, were being screwed—coming and going.

———

In late June 1969, *U.S. News and World Report* did an article on a plan to industrialize and urbanize the Four Corners area. Part of the plan was to build "an ultramodern city of 250,000—'a model city for Indians'—in the Farmington region of New Mexico" so that "all the Indians in the region would be resettled in this city, which was described as 'a novel approach to urban problems' in bringing 'the twentieth century to the Indians.'" I remember talking to Charlie Cambridge about this crazy plan since we were both born in Farmington. I remember him laughing and saying, "Well, what if we don't want it?" I guess it was funny in a way. And, in a way, he was right, as 'Useless News and World Distort' would later muse, "Most Indians, it is believed, would prefer to live on the reservation and commute" to bordertown heaven.

The urban Indian Territory in Greater Farmington was never built. But, of course, the underlying idea to terminate the area's Indian reservations and relocate the Indians so that their land, water, and natural resources could be taken and exploited persisted. The motive for termination and relocation wasn't much different than the geological imperative that created the nineteenth-century Indian Removal Act and the subsequent forced removal of eastern tribes on the Trail of Tears to Indian Territory in Oklahoma. The geological imperative wasn't much different than the motivations behind the Farmington-based Four Corners Regional Commission, which had the Westinghouse Electric Company do a 1969 HUD-funded study on internal imperialism—the "Four Corners Regional Development Study Program: A Study of Development Guidelines Including the Analysis of Economic Potential and the Concept of a New Town for the Four Corners Region."

After I read the monster four-hundred-page report, I learned that Hawley Atkinson was an acting commissioner of the Four Corners Regional Commission. He would later become the senior commissioner and chairman of the Federal Navajo Hopi Indian Relocation Commission charged with the ethnic cleansing of the coal-rich Black Mesa Basin.

And the hits just kept on coming. Westinghouse's next study was for Tucson Gas and Electric Company to justify the construction, operation, and maintenance of the company's controversial powerline across Navajo tribal lands in New Mexico. The powerline and related power plant—the San Juan Power Plant—was part of Western Electrical Supply and Transmission Associates' grand scheme. A regional corporate and governmental trade association, WEST Associates, was also the driving force behind the proposed expansion of the Four Corners Power Plant from five units to eight units in the late sixties and early seventies.

There was also a regional group of coal mining companies, including Utah International, Inc. and Western Coal Company, that operated the Navajo and San Juan power plant mines, respectively. The Tucson Gas and Electric company also co-owned the San Juan mine, San Juan Power Plant, and Four Corners Power Plant.

The constant imperative and relentless drive of the invader beast was formidable. The 1969–71 version of the beast had three heads. Two of the heads were the utility and mining companies. The third and ugliest head to rear up during that particularly dark period of the fossil fuel age was the Federal Bureau of Reclamation (BuRec). As the designated power and water agency of the Department of Interior, BuRec was also a member of WEST Associates.

———

Growing up in Farmington or Totah (Among the Waters), I knew about water and how it was divided. Over two-thirds of the surface water in the state of New Mexico runs through Farmington via the San Juan, Animas, and La Plata rivers, and Glade Arroyo. Upstream from Farmington, Navajo Dam was built at the junction of the San Juan and Pine rivers. The dam created Navajo Lake, flooded the sacred confluence of To Aheedli (Where the Rivers Cross), and extended thirty-five miles beyond the Piedra River Arm of the fifteen-thousand-acre lake into southern Colorado. The BuRec dam and lake complex was built from 1958 to 1962 to store and deliver 508,000 acre-feet per year to the planned 110,000-acre Navajo Indian Irrigation Project south of Farmington. It would also provide water for the coal-fired Four Corners and San Juan electrical generating stations and other downstream municipal, industrial, and agricultural water users in San Juan County, such as Blanco-Bloomfield, Farmington, Kirtland-Fruitland-Waterflow-Hogback, Shiprock, Hammond Project, and the oil and gas industry (even though oil and water still doesn't mix). Upstream from Navajo Dam and Lake is the northern component of BuRec's San Juan-Chama Project, which diverts 110,000 acre-feet of water per year from the Upper San Juan River and its major upstream tributaries across the Continental Divide to the Chama River and Rio Grande basins. The transbasin water diversion project serves Albuquerque, Santa Fe, and other New Mexico urban and rural water users. Near the headwaters of the San Juan River is Project Skywater, a BuRec cloud-seeding operation that began in 1964. Two other Bureau water diversion projects—Gallup-Navajo Project and Animas-La Plata Project—were in the planning stages. These federal projects were planned to serve Gallup, Durango, Cedar Hill, Aztec, Flora Vista, La Plata, several non-Indian settler colony projects, and portions of the Navajo, Southern Ute, and Ute Mountain Ute reservations (primarily the BIA area and agency headquarters or administrative reserves).

———

In my early conspiracy theory days, I was also a beer-and-pizza guy. In the late summer of 1973, I was having a few beers and some pizza at Jack's in Albuquerque and shooting the shit with my old drinking buddy from Farmington, Ricky Anderson, who was a graduating senior at UNM. Ricky's major was civil engineering, so we were soon talking about power and water resource allocation in the San Juan Basin. After I got the last round, he told me to check out the government publications section of the university's engineering library, which had a lot of good information. The next day, I ambled on over to the engineering library. What a find! I owed Ricky a case of beer for that one.

Following the water trail, I found that Secretary of Interior Stewart Udall had colluded with WEST Associates in the mid-sixties to develop a secret plan to reduce the size of the Navajo Indian Irrigation Project from 110,000 acres to 77,000 acres or 62,000 acres so that the "residual water" from the reduced tribal agricultural project could be used for future industrial development in the Four Corners region. The plan was so secret that the Navajo Tribe didn't know about it, even though it was their trust land and water that would be reduced. Despite being legal trust beneficiaries, they were never consulted or informed of the insidious plan to reduce their trust resources by their so-called trustee. In fact, the first time they heard of the plan was when they read about it in the newspapers and, by then, the sordid plan was already developed.

The plan called for Interior's BuRec to "evaluate" the tribal irrigation project since it was in charge of its development (like the agency was in charge of the development of the related Navajo Dam and Lake complex and associated water delivery system to the irrigation project site). Then, based on a projected negative evaluation, the Bureau would recommend project land and water reduction.

Of course, the Navajo Tribe was not appointed as a member of the Bureau's task force for the evaluation of the Navajo Indian Irrigation Project. The Tribe opposed all of this, but it didn't stop the evaluation process from moving forward. The only thing that prevented the departmental implementation of the project acreage reduction plan was that it was illegal. The congressionally authorized size of the tribal irrigation project was 110,000 acres. Although the illegal governmental and corporate plan was withdrawn, the actual process of stealing Indian water for non-Indian energy could still be done without reducing the Indian irrigation project's land size.

At the behest of Secretary Udall, the Bureau of Reclamation amended the purpose of the Navajo Indian Irrigation Project from family farming to corporate farming. The project's cropping patterns changed when it became an agribusiness and the irrigation system also changed from gravity flow to sprinkler, thereby reducing the amount of yearly water diversion from 508,000 acre-feet of water to 370,000 acre-feet; this was further reduced to 330,000 acre-feet per year. This substantial reduction of the project's yearly water diversion also changed the estimated amounts of consumptive use and net depletion that, in turn, changed the estimated return flow from the irrigation project to the San Juan River.

The new project diversion figure was quantifiable. The other figures were just estimates or guesstimates by the BuWreck and could be further manipulated or monkeyed with by agency contractors applying fatally flawed hydrological models or employing unsound modeling methodology. They could even revise the ratios between water usage, depletion, and availability to favor industry over agriculture at will.

The governmental WEST Associates member deliberately overestimated the average annual flow of the San Juan River. This over-allocation of river water and subsequent sharing of shortages would physically reduce the land and water base of the Navajo Indian Irrigation Project. In addition, it intentionally overestimated the quantity and rate of movement of project return flow to the river to further reduce the physical resource base of the tribal irri-gation project.

The deceit and treachery behind the planned reduction and changes in irrigable acreage and acre-feet of the Navajo Indian Irrigation Project was to "create" more water for more coal develop-ment. Concomitantly, the deceitful and treacherous overestimation of the quantity and rate of migration of the project's return flow to the River San Juan (aka River Udall) was another form of reduction. The false and fraudulent overestimations were just lies to steal more Navajo water so that more coal could be mined for electrical gen-eration, or gasification, or liquefaction—or all three inappropriate coal conversion technologies.

They didn't call Secretary Udall the "Czar of the River" for noth-ing. In 1967, the Secretary got Congress to certify his predetermined hydrological assessment that there were one hundred thousand acre-feet of water per year in the San Juan River Basin available for municipal and industrial uses. Congress then approved a water ser-vice contract for Utah International, Inc. to use forty-four thousand acre-feet of water per year from the San Juan River for industrial purposes, such as coal conversion. It also approved a water service contract for the Public Service Company of New Mexico (PNM) to use an annual sixteen thousand acre-feet from the river for the proposed San Juan Power Plant.

Utah International also had a water supply contract with the State of New Mexico to use fifty-five thousand acre-feet of water from the river for industrial purposes such as—all together now—coal conversion. It then leased or sold most of its water supply to the Arizona Public Service Company (APS) for use in the Four Corners Power Plant. They also committed to lease or sell most of the remaining water supply (from the state contract, not the federal contract) to PNM for the proposed San Juan generating station. In addition to selling coal for APS to use in the Four Corners gener-ating station, Utah International committed to selling coal from its Navajo Mine to PNM for its proposed San Juan Power Plant. This dedicated coal would supplement the coal mined by Western Coal Company at its proposed San Juan Mine.

Utah International served as a primary and secondary coal supplier to area power plants and engaged in industrial water speculating on the San Juan River. It was a mining company, not an electrical generating company, a gasification company, or a liquefaction company. It got water rights from the state and the Feds for coal conversion purposes. However, instead of doing the coal conversion itself, it leased or sold the contract water to coal conversion companies like APS, PNM, and WESCO.

———

I was also a beer-and-burger guy back in the day. In the early fall of 1973, I was having a B&B at Rosie's Cantina in Algodones when Dr. Harvey Headpounder came in with his Billy Jack hat and Foster Grant shades. I was expecting him. A week earlier, he had called me collect from the Bisti Trading Post to ask about meeting me in private. I tentatively agreed to meet him at a neutral site, Rosie's, since I did not know him or what he wanted. The next day, he sent me a telegram from the Western Union office in Farmington to confirm the date, time, and place of our meeting. We chatted, chewed, and quaffed from noon to two in the morning at the Algodones watering hole on old Highway 85.

He said he was from the Bisti Badlands. He went to Navajo Mission in Farmington. After he graduated, he joined the paramilitary North American Indian Liberation Front and ran guns to the Native underground resistance that was waging hot wars of liberation throughout Turtle Island in the late fifties and early sixties. After two hundred successful gun-running missions, he enrolled at UCLA in Westwood, where he eventually got his post-doctorate in political geography. He then taught Indian liberation studies at Occidental College in Pasadena before being blacklisted as a communist. Finally, he went back to Farmington and lived under a mosquito-infested bridge along Glade Arroyo until 1967. He hung out on the streets of Farmington from 1968 to 1971. During that foggy period, he frequented the El Vacito bar on West Main and got to know some rather interesting characters like a woman named Louise who lived down by the river.

When Dr. Headpounder got up to use the bathroom, I sat there wondering where this conversation was going. He came back and continued, "Anyway, Louise knew a man named Herbert who used to work for a tall white man named Hank, the minerals supervisor for the Navajo Tribe in Window Rock. After his five-year contract was up, Hank resigned as tribal minerals supervisor and set up a private geological survey business in Farmington and Houston. His new business, or front, was headquartered in the posh Petroleum Plaza office building in Farmington and the Houston connection had something to do with Texas Eastern Transmission Corporation of Houston." Harvey stopped and took another sip of his beer. Then he started again. "What all this has to do with me is that Hank and his associates are in the unscrupulous business of coal and resource speculating on the so-called public domain in the Bisti area. Where I grew up and where my people are. Hank and his boys are geologists and they know the Bisti-Chaco-Star Lake region is full of coal. They want to open the coal region for development by brokering leases for big mining and utility companies interested in exploiting the area. And they want to get rich as the chosen gatekeepers to the treasures. It is every prospector's wet dream."

Dr. Harvey paused, not for effect, but to refill his frosted mug. Then he proceeded, "They do this by buying low and selling high. The coal properties. They flip them. That's how they do it. One could easily become a millionaire if you know what you're doing. For example, they can lease a parcel or tract of federal coal resource land from the BLM for, say, twenty-five dollars an acre, sit on it for a while, renew it if they have to, then, when the market conditions are ripe, sell or assign it at a super high profit to a major company like Utah International or PNM, and last but not least, be sure to retain a percentage of overriding royalties. Of course, they buy up blocks of land, not just parcels or tracts. It's pretty much the same thing amateur geologist and former New Mexico Governor Tom

Bolack of Farmington did in the forties and fifties, except he did it with cheap government oil and gas leases, not coal leases. He later sold a lot of his leases in the San Juan Basin to Delhi-Taylor Oil Company. The oil development south of Farmington in the sixties also increased access to the Bisti Badlands via the new Bisti bridge and highway. Geopolitically speaking, infrastructure accommodates development."

Rosie yelled out, "last call," which was all too soon followed by "closing time." As the lights rudely came on and the music abruptly stopped, we had to wrap it up quickly. "Another thing, before I leave," Harvey said, "one of Hank's buddies, Elliott of Farmington, is in the related—and it is related—business of buying and selling state coal permits and leases. Like the leasable federal land and mineral inholdings within the Eastern Navajo Agency, there is a lot of leasable state land and resource inholdings within the exterior boundaries of the New Mexico Navajo Checkerboard Area. So, this white geologist coal scam is both federal and state. And my poor people, who live on the land that is being leased right out from under them, don't even know what's going on. Do you think you can help us, brother?" I told him that I would do what I can, even though I was already stretched to the max.

When I got back to my base in Albuquerque, I expanded the scope of the UNM Navajo Coal Gasification Project to properly integrate the Bisti coal leasing issue. It was an integral part of the larger geopolitical landscape, so brilliantly illuminated by Dr. Harvey Headpounder in a follow-up phone call to our rendezvous at Rosie's. Enlightened by the master, I now saw the coal trend extending from Nenahnezad to Burnham to Bisti to Star Lake and beyond. The coal trail (or strip mine alley, as Dr. Headpounder called it) followed the areally connected Fruitland, Navajo, Bisti, and Star Lake coalfields. This new geophysical lens clearly revealed the spatial coal connections that modeled my research.

Harvey also said that geopolitics is always about control of territory. We were losing territorial control over much of our tribal homeland—both on and off the reservation. "It is still part of our homeland," he said. "Our land, water, and natural resources in the New Mexico portion of the Navajo reservation and the entire Checkerboard Area are in great danger of being taken over and super-exploited by powerful outside forces driven by external pressures exerted from the loci of wheeling marketplaces. If we lose control over northern and eastern Navajo," Harvey said, "the whole area from Shiprock to Torreon to Crownpoint will look like Pittsburgh in less than a decade. The leasing is the first part of the industrial invasion. In the real-life context of tribal homeland defense," he said, "we, as a tribal people and nation, have to take a stand. We have to take a stand. Or else."

Harvey was a big-picture guy but he needed specific details. That's what I was for. To get intel for the coming Coal War.

If victory was the goal, we had to know our enemy better. After doing some digging, I found out that "Herbert" was Herbert Tsosie, who now worked for WESCO (of which Texas Eastern Transmission Corporation was a part). I also learned that "Hank" was Henry Pohlmann of Pohlmann and Associates in Farmington and Houston. "Elliott" was Elliott Riggs, who used to work for Texaco, Inc., the company that opened the giant Aneth Oil Field. Herbert Tsosie used to work for the Navajo Tribal Minerals Department and Hank Pohlmann and Elliott Riggs were knowledgeable and experienced petroleum geologists. They and their colleagues and associates were very familiar with the San Juan Basin.

I also researched the history and status of the state and federal coal leasing programs in northwestern New Mexico, with a particular emphasis on non-competitive or preference right leasing on state and federal lands in San Juan, McKinley, Valencia, and Sandoval counties, where most of the regional government-controlled coal resources were located.

My research revealed that Texas Eastern Transmission Corporation (and its subsidiary Fannin Square Corporation and its affiliates Eastern Associates Properties Corporation and Eastern Gas and Fuel Associates) had acquired most of their state and federal coal leases in the Bisti-Star Lake region from 1968 to 1973.

Other state and federal coal leaseholders in the region included the usual suspects such as Utah International, Inc., El Paso Natural Gas Company, Consolidation Coal Company, Western Coal Company, plus a whole slew of other companies, corporations, fronts, and speculators.

Besides Hank and Elliott, there were other state and federal coal permit and lease speculators like Leland Hodges and Ben Donegan of Leonard Resources of Dallas-Fort Worth who had intriguing ties to Peabody Coal Company, Thermal Energy Company, Cherokee-Pittsburgh Coal Mining Company, Santa Fe Industries, and Gulf Oil Company.

———

During spring break in 1974, I met with Harvey at the Cuban Café in Cuba. We talked over heaping plates of huevos rancheros, fresh torts (tortillas), and endless cups of hot black coffee. I told him that my preliminary research indicated that there was a shit storm coming. There were over 150 approved state coal leases (mostly non-competitive or preference right leases) covering tens of thousands of acres overlying several billion tons of strip-minable coal. Most of the leases issued by the New Mexico State Land Office conflicted with "illegal" Navajo-occupied lands in the checkerboarded Eastern Navajo Agency. There were twenty-six pending federal preference right lease applications (PLRA) covering seventy-five thousand acres overlying 2.2 billion tons of strippable coal. Most, if not all, of the PLRA applications proposed to be issued by the BLM conflicted with "illegal" Navajo-inhabited lands in the split-estated Eastern Navajo Agency. This governmental and corporate leasing frenzy represented the beginning of the coal rush in the New Mexico Navajo Checkerboard Area, and there would be much more to come.

Now, on his twentieth cup of coffee, Harvey asked me to take him back to the beginning of the current coal leasing frenzy.

I told him the aggressive coal leasing began in 1964 when Stewart Udall issued a public land order opening selected sections

118

of the Checkerboard Area (which had been set aside for exclusive Navajo use by previous secretarial public land orders) for exclusive non-Indian mineral exploration and development under the federal Mineral Leasing Act of 1920. That same year, WEST Associates (another evil brainchild of Stew Udall and his industry co-conspirators in 1961) announced a twenty-year plan to construct twenty electrical generating power plants in the West. The regional governmental and corporate trade association also announced plans to expand the Four Corners Power Plant from three units to five units. The planned construction of the multi-unit San Juan Power Plant was also part of the new power plant development scheme. In fact, PNM president D.W. Reeves was the first WEST Associates president. To neatly accommodate the planned expansion of the Four Corners generating station, the Navajo Mine lease was expanded from twenty-four thousand coal acres to thirty-one thousand coal acres. Western Coal Company was actively exploring for future coal supply reserves on government land in close proximity to the planned San Juan generating station site.

Harvey now switched from endless cups of coffee to chain-smoking complimentary Cuban Café cigars. I continued.

Besides the Four Corners and San Juan power plants, WEST Associates members planned to expand the Reid Gardner Power Plant near the Moapa Southern Paiute reservation in Nevada and the existing Cholla Power Plant near Joseph City, which got its coal from the McKinley Mine near Black Hat. There were also plans by the twenty-three-member public and private utility group to build power plants near Page and Paiute Farms on the Navajo reservation in Arizona and Utah, Kaiparowits and Huntington in Utah, and Bullhead City near the Arizona-Nevada border. Some of the proposed power plants would be mine-mouth facilities. Others would use coal mined elsewhere and transported by railroad or water slurry pipelines. That's where the Black Mesa Basin and portions of the San Juan Basin come in. And the geostrategic Bisti-Star Lake coal region as part of the San Juan embayment.

Soon, lunch was served. Harvey and I had a couple of bowls of fiery green chile stew accompanied by crisp sopies (sopapillas) and real Mexican cocoa. After lunch, I got really sleepy and wanted to take an afternoon siesta. After half a pot of strong black coffee, I perked up and continued.

WEST Associates got some of their coal supply and most of their water in the fifties and sixties. Then, they got their water storage and delivery systems in place at Navajo Dam, Navajo Lake, Glen Canyon Dam, and Lake Powell in the sixties. They also got some of their coal supply committed at Bisti-Star Lake but had no transportation infrastructure to get it to market and no coal export facilities.

They now had a so-called geo-demographic or human overburden problem—all the problematic Navajos sitting on top of the coal seams. Strip miners deal with overburden by physically removing whatever is on top to get at the coal below. In the case of the Navajo overburden, this involved forced human removal. The BLM had done a study last year called the "Navajo Indian Status Study in Northwestern New Mexico," which set into motion the Navajo human overburden removal process. The Bureau's Farmington Resource area office had already carved up the Checkerboard Area into two planning units—San Juan and Chaco. They had identified the Navajos standing in the way of their coal leasing program and defined them as unauthorized occupants or squatters on the public domain. Their human inventory or body count enumerated eight thousand Navajo squatters. It was all about getting access to the undeveloped coal leases—that was the underlying reason for the land-and-people plans.

The mining leases were the linchpin for a lot of this planned power plant development. In order to mine coal on the leases, they obviously planned to remove the Navajo overburden. To transport the mined coal to market, they intended to remove more Navajo overburden from the coal transportation rights-of-way to establish a web of railroad spurs and haulage roads. That was the genesis of the coal leasing frenzy.

Anyway, I need to make a solid historical case for the people who live on the land. Even the BLM says that we've lived on this land since the late 1400s. Except for the Long Walk period of 1864–68, the folks have continuously inhabited this region for five hundred years. We were here long before the Spanish, the Mexicans, and the Americans. And certainly before the BLM. We aren't squatters on our own land. They are the squatters on our land.

"Fucking A right!" Harvey shouted. With that, we ordered supper in the form of two giant beef-and-bean burritos—each the size of a burly truck driver's forearm—smothered, in fact, swimming in deep pungent red chile. There was also the bottomless pitcher of Fidel's finest homemade lemonade. Is this stuff legal? For dessert, we had the house natillas (which, incidentally, was on the house).

The best part of the day came when Dr. Harvey said that he believed this whole thing—the subject matter of our dialogue—was a coal *AND* water conspiracy. Finally, I was not alone. We agreed to meet again soon.

———

Then, in late April, Farmington happened—again, and I was diverted.

During that time, the BLM published a follow-up study on the pressing issue of "widespread" unauthorized Navajo occupancy on national natural resource lands in the San Juan and Chaco planning units in the Farmington Resource Area. The study reported that 2,500 of the eight thousand unauthorized Navajo occupants on the BLM-administered public domain in northwestern New Mexico were trespassing on BLM-leased or leasable mineral resource lands. Gulf Oil Company, representing the corporate leaseholders, supported the termination and cessation of "Indian occupancy trespass." Its subsidiary, Pittsburgh-Midway Coal Mining Company, called for the permanent removal of "Navajo squatters." Even the BLM discussed a plan for "the mandatory relocation" of unauthorized occupants "located on high-value mineral lands or other lands needed for BLM programs." As part of the BLM coal leasing program, such "other lands" could be vacated and ethnically cleansed for the suitable siting of non-Indian coal transportation facilities and white coalfield trash trailer parks. The BLM further discussed the necessity of taking "legal action beyond the scope of administrative procedures" in order "to cause eviction." It also discussed "the disposition of occupants" following ejection from the BLM-authorized coal "overlay" zone.

Then, in early September, NIYC happened, and I was diverted again, but not quite as much.

In October, Gerry and I met with a BLM liaison official at the office in a good-faith effort to sensitize him to the life-and-death issue of forced Indian removal. Gerry, a Cherokee, told him about the genocide of the Trail of Tears. I told him, as a Navajo, about the holocaust of the Long Walk. He was sympathetic but ultimately did not have the power to change the situation.

I tried to contact Harvey before the meeting, but he was unreachable. He had told me that he worked as a night watchman at the La Vida Mission at Lake Valley but when I called the mission, the Seventh Day Adventist Church lady said that she never heard of him. During the winter break, I went to Bisti but the elders at the trading post told me that they had not seen their native son since 1959 when he hitchhiked to a continental meeting at Onondaga.

I wasn't sure what was happening. In the movement, people come and go all the time—but not like that. I missed Harvey, if in fact he did exist. I was pretty sure he did. JoAllan thought I was crazy. In any case, the struggle continued and I kept my shoulder to the wheel.

In 1975, Texas Eastern Transmission Corporation confirmed rumors that it was planning to build a complex of mine-mouth coal gasification plants in the Bisti-Chaco area. In 1976, Santa Fe Railroad Company filed an application with the federal Interstate Commerce Commission for a permit to construct and operate a railroad to transport coal out of the Bisti-Star Lake mining region. In 1977, the Public Service Company of New Mexico announced plans to build a large mine-mouth coal-fired electrical generating power plant and a "possible" new town near Bisti. That year, the

BLM held a scoping meeting on the preparation of environmental impact statements for the proposed railroad project and related coal mining activities.

At the public meeting, I blasted the whole damn thing—the leasing, the planned mining, the railroad, the power plant, the powerlines, the "possible" new town, the possible coal gasification plants, the relocation planning. The entire strip-off scheme. Influenced to the core by Dr. Headpounder's intellectual legacy, I now saw the larger picture and took the long view of the harsh geopolitical terrain and the constancy of invasion. In 1978, the BLM issued the draft environmental impact statement (EIS) for the proposed strip-and-ship project. At the BLM draft EIS public hearings, I charged the agency with crimes against humanity and nature in its programmatic mission to clear the Bisti-Star Lake region for large-scale coal leasing and development. The BLM, I testified, was an agent of genocide.

Then, in early January 1979, the American Indian Environmental Council happened, and I was diverted yet again.

CHAPTER 5

URANIUM IS GENOCIDE

In July 1973, my uncle Fleming Begaye set up a meeting in Gallup for me to meet with Fred Johnson, who was recently appointed as the new deputy director of DNA People's Legal Services. Although Fred and I knew of each other, we had never actually met. Fleming was so well-connected and good at setting up meetings like this. A month earlier, he set up a meeting between then-DNA People's Legal Services executive director Leo Haven and me in Window Rock to discuss critical Navajo tribal government development and reform issues. Anyway, my meeting with Fred took place in the famed lobby of the luxurious El Rancho Hotel—Charm of Yesterday, Convenience of Tomorrow—on historic Route 66. Per Uncle Fleming's agenda, Fred and I each discussed our work and how we could work together.

After we talked about Black Mesa and Burnham (Mitch Fowler already had a working relationship with DNA in both affected or soon-to-be-affected areas), we talked about Tucson Gas and Electric (TG&E). Although DNA and IAE were both working on the TG&E issue, we did not work together—primarily because we were each working on different aspects of the issue. DNA was working on the legal aspect, while IAE was working on the community education and organizing aspect. I had invited IAE TG&E project group leader Robert Tohe to attend our networking meeting so that we three could more effectively collaborate and coordinate our work on the TG&E issue which was coming to a head in the Navajo Tribal Council chambers. Fred and I then turned to the matter of the Exxon uranium lease. I was only vaguely aware of the lease issue, so Fred briefed me.

He said the Exxon Corporation wanted a big uranium lease that would span from Red Rock to Toadlena to Shiprock to Beclabito to Cove. They wanted to explore, mine, and mill uranium within this huge 400,000-acre area they hoped to lease. Like my mother Rose, Fleming was originally from Red Rock, where a lot of radioactive uranium mining occurred from the early fifties to the late sixties. Now, many former uranium miners were getting sick and dying from cancer and leukemia due to their chronic exposure to deadly radiation in the uranium mines. Fred said that Richard Hughes from Shiprock DNA was trying to get compensation for the uranium radiation victims, but there were no radiation exposure compensation laws on the books. The Red Rock and Cove communities were also jointly working with several congressmen and senators to get federal legislation passed to compensate the victims and their families. Fred said that there should be no more uranium leasing and development until the radiation victims and their families are compensated—or until there was a cure for cancer, leukemia, and other radiation-caused sicknesses. When Fred said no more uranium leasing and development, he specifically meant Exxon.

Despite our best organizing efforts, Navajo Tribal Chairman Peter MacDonald got the tribal council to pass a resolution approving TG&E's powerline right-of-way lease. That was in early August. Then, as he did with the proposed TG&E project, Chairman MacDonald got the council to pass a resolution authorizing him, as chairman, to personally negotiate the proposed uranium exploration, mining, and milling lease with Exxon. That was in late August. August was a good month for the bad guys—MacDonald, TG&E, and Exxon—and a bad month for the good guys: IAE, DNA, and the grassroots.

In mid-September, I met with Fred at the Indian Village at the New Mexico State Fair in Albuquerque to discuss strategy. On

TG&E, DNA would legally challenge the right-of-way lease. On Exxon, Fred, Elmer Barber, Taylor Dixon, and other local community leaders in the proposed lease area would begin working with the people who lived on the land.

Although I was back in school, I was able to do a little research on uranium leasing in the Navajo reservation and checkerboard area. I showed Fred a series of maps where there were at least ten large uranium exploration leases issued in the New Mexico and Arizona portions of the rez from 1966 to 1971 and pointed out that three of the leases appeared to be located within the now-proposed Exxon uranium lease. In addition, there were significant uranium lease sale activities in the checkerboard and split-estate areas of the Church Rock and Crownpoint communities in the Eastern Navajo Agency. "Something major is happening," I told Fred, "and the proposed 625-square mile Exxon uranium lease was only part of it."

In mid-September, JoAllan took me to the annual Laguna Pueblo Feast Day. She also took me to see the Grand Canyon-sized Jackpile Mine at Paguate. The uranium strip mine was so big and so close to the village that I almost fell in. Later, I found out that it was the nation's largest open-pit uranium mine. JoAllan also heard about deep underground uranium mining slated to begin on Mount Taylor. I knew that Mount Taylor was sacred to the Navajos and I trusted that it was sacred to the nearby Laguna and Acoma Pueblos as well. And to Zuni Pueblo of which she was a tribal member. I immediately had visions of us working together as a Navajo-Pueblo team to protect and defend Mount Taylor and other common sacred lands. There was so much work to do!

I was still in school, so I couldn't do that much. I did, however, do a little more research on some of the Navajo uranium leases.

Two of the 1968 leases were located in the still-uranium-rich Lukachukai and Carrizo mountains. The Syracuse Mine in the Lukachukai Mountains had something to do with the US War Department's Manhattan Project, and I knew the Carrizo Mountains were extensively mined for the War Department's Trinity Project. My father Alden was born at the foot of the Carrizos, and several of his half-brothers worked in the wartime uranium and vanadium mines in the early forties. The 1968 lease in the Lukachukais was held by the Kerr-McGee Corporation. I didn't know who McGee was but found out that Kerr was US Senator Robert Kerr who was then president of the corporation.

The Kerr-McGee Corporation (KMC) also owned Kerr-McGee Oil Industries, Inc., which had begun mining uranium in the Lukachukais in 1952. By 1955, it was operating sixty mines in the mountain range south of Cove and Red Rock. The uranium was mined for national defense purposes, or so claimed the military-industrial complex. I, of course, thought the Cold War-era uranium mining in the Lukachukais was another wave of governmental and corporate invasion and exploitation. And it was—but there was more.

Based on my continuing research on KMC, it was hard to believe the 'coincidence' that President Lyndon Johnson (a close friend and colleague of Senator Kerr) would appoint former Kerr-McGee attorney and Senator Kerr's close friend, Clark Clifford as Secretary of Defense. There was too much illicit intersection and confluence of special political and business interests here.

Interior Secretary Stewart Udall also approved the 1968 leases as well as Kerr-McGee's 1966 uranium lease or leases in the Church Rock area of the prolific Grants Mineral Belt (aka Grants Uranium Belt). Hank Pohlmann was also Navajo tribal minerals supervisor from 1963 to 1968. Speaking of Honest Hank, I continued my research into Kerr-McGee's penetration strategy.

———

All the way back in 1949, the F.A. Sitton Company acquired a number of uranium mining leases in the Lukachukais. The F.A. Sitton Company then reorganized into F.A. Sitton, Inc. and acquired a lease for a large uranium mill in Shiprock. F.A. Sitton, Inc. then reorganized and became Navajo Uranium Company. Then Navajo Uranium Company assigned its uranium mining and milling leases to Kerr-McGee Oil Industries, Inc., a subsidiary of Kerr-McGee Corporation.

At this point, I was starting to get a little confused. So, I went to Henry's and had a hamburger, coke, and fries. After lunch, I began sorting things out. We were looking at three uranium exploration and production periods.

The first period was the wartime mining in the Carrizos that was conducted by Carrizo Uranium Company and Vanadium Corporation of America (VCA). I didn't know much about the Syracuse Mine in the Lukachukais and would have to follow up on that. However, the Union Mines Development Corporation did conduct post-mining exploration in the Carrizos. The uranium and vanadium ore mined in the Carrizos (and possibly at Syracuse Mine in the Lukachukais) was milled at Vanadium Corporation of America's Smelter Mountain Mill in Durango until the end of World War II in 1945.

The second period was from 1946 to 1968 (or 1971). Mining in the Carrizos was done by VCA, with milling done at VCA's Smelter Mountain Mill until 1963. Mining in the Lukachukais was done by Kerr-McGee Oil Industries, Inc., with milling done at Smelter Mountain Mill until 1954. Mining in Sanostee and other Northern Navajo Agency uranium mining districts was done by companies other than VCA and KMC, with milling done at Smelter Mountain Mill until 1954 or 1963—that was another thing to follow up on.

The US Atomic Energy Commission (AEC) built a uranium ore buying station in Shiprock in 1952 and operated the station until 1954, when Kerr-McGee built its uranium mill in Shiprock. KMC operated its mill until 1963, processing uranium ore mined from KMC's mines in the Lukachukais and possibly non-KMC mines in Sanostee and other Shiprock Agency mining districts (including non-VCA mines in the Carrizos). That same year, VCA also closed its Smelter Mountain Mill to take over KMC's mill in Shiprock, which it operated from 1963 to 1968 when it closed. The VCA mill in Shiprock milled uranium from VCA and non-VCA mines in the Carrizos, KMC's mines in the Lukachukais, and non-KMC mines in Sanostee and other Northern Agency mining districts. I didn't know much about uranium mining and milling in the Shiprock Agency mining districts from 1969 to 1971—another thing I would have to follow up on.

The third period started in about 1972 and was ongoing. The Atomic Energy Commission was on the way out and Exxon et al. were on the way in. Most of the area explored, mined, and milled from the early forties to the late sixties (or early seventies) was located within the now-proposed Exxon uranium lease area. There were many more questions that remained unanswered. What about the oil on the lease? Why was Kerr-McGee Oil Industries, Inc. in the uranium business? Was there a larger energy agenda at play? Why did VCA merge with Foote Mineral Company in 1967? Who the hell was Foote? Was there something else afoot? Suddenly, a rare Lobo Firefly flew by, then another, then a whole armada. Oh shit, it was past midnight and the moon was out. I grabbed a slice of pizza at Casa Luna and went home.

The next morning, I got up and went to class but couldn't concentrate on the lecture. So, I took the bus to Western Skies on East Central, then to Nine Mile Hill on West Central, and finally back to the bus stop at Knadjian's, where I got off. It was clear now. I had to widen the scope of my research investigation.

I knew Kerr-McGee and Exxon were both in the oil business, and I wanted to follow their oil trail on Navajo, particularly in the uranium and oil-rich Four Corners area. However, before I got in too deep on this latest research tangent, I thought I would treat my long-suffering girlfriend, JoAllan, to dinner at our favorite neighborhood restaurant, Indrapura. It was the least I could do. Being on a twenty-four seven movement track could be hard on a relationship. So, we went to the unique Dutch Indonesian eatery, which was centered between Jack's and Okie's—the eighth and ninth wonders of the world. JoAllan had the chicken curry or curry chicken. I had the usual—Dutch meatballs with to-die-for-Indonesian rice. As we dined and shared a pot of house hallucinogenic tea, we talked about library research. JoAllan, a master's degree candidate, had a lot more academic knowledge and experience in that specialized information science field than I did. I was just some guy off the street. Almost an MA, she went on about how Arizona State's Hayden Library was much better organized than New Mexico's Zimmerman Library. But Tempe didn't have an Indrapura. So, Zimmerman it was!

JoAllan expertly advised that I check the stacks at Zimmerman. She then told me which level and stack I should go to, which I wrote on a napkin for future reference. After dinner, we went to the very young Pointer Sisters concert at Popejoy Hall on campus. The resounding two-hour performance ended with the future Los Angeles Lakers—Showtime Lakers—theme song, "I'm So Excited." Our exciting evening ended later with a couple of nightcaps at the Pow Wow Club. Then, it was back to my apartment on Sycamore where I carefully tucked the valuable note-scribbled napkin under the pillow before the nimble fingers of sleep gently overtook me, gently overtook me. . . .

The next day, I went to the tower that held the stacks. Consulting the napkin only once, I found the right level or floor and stack with relative ease. Surveying the aisles of impressive holdings, I sensed that I was getting closer to establishing the relevant but so far overlooked oil connection, which I was sure was part of the recent uranium resource play by Kerr-McGee, Exxon, and other diversified energy principals. I found a map showing four major oilfields—Rattlesnake, Tocito Dome, Table Mesa, and Hogback— located within the proposed Exxon uranium lease. It also showed that the giant Diné Bi Keyah (DBK) Oil Field in the Lukachukais was leased by Kerr-McGee Oil Industries, Inc. and Humble Oil and Refining Company (which had recently become Exxon). According to the map, one of the 1968 uranium leases was located in the vicinity of the co-leased DBK Oil Field.

For the next week, I was immersed in the stacks.

———

In 1962, Clark Clifford (then just a Washington DC attorney) approached then-Navajo Tribal Chairman Paul Jones to approve a "negotiated" lease in the Lukachukais for an "undisclosed principal." Negotiated leases are not competitive—they are preferential right leases. The undisclosed principal was the party refusing to disclose its name. Chairman Jones referred the matter to Norman Littell, the tribal attorney, who advised against negotiated leasing. He favored competitive leasing.

All of these men had a history—direct or indirect. Clark Clifford was a close friend and colleague of then-Vice President Lyndon Johnson, who was, in turn, a close friend and colleague of Senator Robert Kerr, the president of Kerr-McGee Corporation and owner of Kerr-McGee Oil Industries, Inc. Before Lyndon Johnson was vice president and president, he was a US House Representative. As Chairman of the House Subcommittee on Naval Petroleum Reserves, Representative Johnson supported Standard Oil Company of California's proposal to illegally lease oil from Elk Hills Naval Petroleum Reserve in California.

Before Norman Littell was Navajo tribal attorney, he was the US Assistant Attorney General who investigated the oil lease proposal and declared it "illegal and invalid." Littell's legal opinion soon led to the cancellation of the proposed lease and apparent sweetheart contract between Standard Oil and Johnson. Congressman Johnson unsuccessfully protested the lease cancellation to the US Attorney General. Suffice to say, LBJ never forgot or forgave Littell. The Elk Hills Naval Petroleum Reserve was also a major federal-corporate crime scene in the infamous Teapot Dome Scandal.

When Littell met with Mr. Clifford, he asked for the name of the undisclosed principal. Clifford said that he did not have the authority to disclose the name, but he would seek such authority. Clifford later disclosed the name of Kerr-McGee Oil Industries, Inc. After acknowledging the name of the company, Littell still advised against a negotiated lease in favor of a competitive lease. Clifford added that the company had given him stock and might give Littell stock if he cooperated. Littell later said that he rejected Clifford's offer.

In 1963, Raymond Nakai of Lukachukai was elected as the new tribal chairman. In his campaign, Mr. Nakai promised that he would fire Norman Littell as tribal attorney. Tribal Chairman Nakai appointed a new advisory committee to the Navajo tribal council, which was authorized to act on behalf of the tribal council when the council was not in session. In 1963 and 1965, Chairman Nakai and his appointed advisory committee granted two leases to Kerr-McGee Oil Industries, Inc. It was unknown whether the leases were negotiated or competitive leases (they were probably negotiated leases since Hank Pohlmann was Navajo tribal minerals supervisor at the time). In 1966, Kerr-McGee Oil Industries, Inc. discovered oil on one of its leaseholds in the Lukachukais (Pohlmann said that the company discovered oil in 1965). It was the richest oil discovery in the state of Arizona, but the company did not announce the discovery. In fact, it didn't even inform the Navajo Tribe (except for maybe Pohlmann). The oil well was capped and the discovery was kept secret. In the meantime, Kerr-McGee Oil Industries, Inc. applied for additional leases in the area, which were granted by Tribal Chairman Nakai and the advisory committee. In early 1967, Kerr-McGee Oil Industries, Inc. announced a major oil discovery on its expanded leaseholdings in the Lukachukais. Several weeks later, Norman Littell was forced to resign as tribal attorney.

In 1963, Lyndon Johnson became the president and Secretary of Interior Stewart Udall suspended Norman Littell's contract as Navajo tribal attorney. Mr. Littell unsuccessfully appealed Secretary Udall's decision. In 1967, the Supreme Court declined to review Littell's appeal. In 1964, Stewart Udall was reappointed as Secretary of Interior and approved a number of uranium and oil leases in the Lukachukais for the Kerr-McGee empire. In a statement to the Senate Subcommittee on Indian Affairs, former Navajo tribal attorney Norman Littell stated that "there is overwhelming evidence of President Johnson's personal knowledge of Navajo affairs. [He] sent a personal telegram of congratulations to the Navajos when the tribe received from Kerr-McGee a check for uranium interests."

The Kerr-McGee monopoly continued in 1967 with another oil lease in the Lukachukais granted to Kerr-McGee Oil Industries, Inc. This forty-seven-thousand-acre area under lease became known as the Diné Bi Keyah Oil Field. It was "Arizona's largest oil field" and variously described as "most prolific," "most exotic," and "unique." Humble Oil and Refining Company—which would later become the Exxon Corporation—also drilled for oil and helium gas in the area.

———

My weeklong immersion session in the stacks was quite useful for gathering the available information. There were some rather frustrating gaps and I didn't have the means or resources to go to ASU's Hayden Library to fill them in. Plus, there were new areas that needed to be researched, such as the geological distribution and outcroppings of extended major coalfield areas located within the proposed Exxon lease boundaries.

I was particularly struck by the enormous size of the planned concession of Navajo land. It was larger than most Indian reservations in the state of New Mexico! The lease proposal also mentioned uranium "and" associated minerals.

By this time, I was doing Eastern Navajo coal research for Harvey Headpounder. That's when I ran across a BLM land and mineral exchange document stating that the Public Service Company of New Mexico was studying the possibility of siting coal and nuclear power plants at Bisti. A nuclear power plant needs uranium to operate, and there might be an available supply of uranium right across the Chaco Wash in a few years. Now things were starting to fall into place, I thought.

Peter MacDonald was also making the rounds in the fall of 1973. In his public statements, he was anti-BIA but pro-Exxon. Anti-colonialism but pro-exploitation?! MacDonald didn't want any BIA involvement in his personal lease negotiations with Exxon. From a fiery red nationalist perspective, his position sounded great, even revolutionary—the BIA was always interfering with Indian self-determination initiatives. But what Mac and Exxon really didn't want was for the BIA to do an environmental impact statement (or statements) on their ecocidal uranium project.

How are they going to do that? By demanding that the BIA area director, the Commissioner of Indian Affairs, and the Secretary of Interior waive the statutory requirement that they must review, and ultimately approve, a negotiated lease. With no federal action on the tribal-corporate deal, it would be self-approving.

If the BIA, Indian Commissioner, and Interior caved into MacDonald and Exxon's demands, how does a federal approval requirement circumvent the EIS process? To answer that, let's first look at the National Environmental Policy Act (NEPA). In procedural terms, it says that a lead agency like BIA must conduct adequate draft and final environmental impact statements before a record of decision is issued for a proposed project like uranium exploration and development. A major federal action (like an approval) is required for any proposed project that will likely have a significant impact on the quality of the human environment. The EIS studies are intended to rigorously analyze the projected environmental impacts for decision-making purposes. Under the law, the BIA and Department of Interior's required project approval constituted a major federal action that would trigger the EIS process. However, MacDonald and company wanted to be above the law. If the federal approval requirement was waived in the interest of tribal radioactive sovereignty, then the EIS requirement would be waived. Mac and Exxon wanted to prevent an EIS study not only because it was costly and time-consuming but an inadequately prepared EIS would be subject to effective legal challenges, which could further delay or even kill the proposed project. That's why Mac and Exxon didn't want an EIS.

The project's proponents claimed that the proposed action wasn't really a lease—it was a joint venture. Yet, the document I saw clearly showed that the actual business arrangement was an unequal partnership whereby Exxon would be the majority or dominant party and the Navajo Tribe would be the minority or submissive partner. As the dominant party, Exxon would have ultimate control of the uranium enterprise on ceded Navajo tribal lands.

———

Now, back to the past to look and understand the present and future.

Despite his reputation, Norman Littell was certainly no angel. In the mid-fifties, he and his oil and gas consultants—Martin Toscan Bennett and Associates of Washington, DC—tried a similar end-around of existing federal Indian law in a dubious tribal partnership agreement with Delhi-Taylor Oil Corporation. Instead of seeking exclusion from NEPA compliance, they were trying to get an exemption from applicable national fluid mineral exploration and production regulation statutes, which they felt were too restrictive. They even tried to legislatively eliminate the veto power of the Interior Secretary, who previously denied their questionable joint venture proposal that was largely based on regressive withdrawal programming or piecemeal termination. No doubt inspiring future Exxon lease negotiators, the Delhi-Taylor deal covered a lot of tribal territory. Over five million acres. That was more than one-third of the entire reservation. Not only was the prized territory rich in oil and gas but it was rich in coal and uranium as well. Kind of like the Exxon land and resource grab now in progress.

I didn't know the particulars of Navajo tribal actions on authorizing lease negotiations, so I did some legislative research on the subject, specifically Exxon lease negotiations.

On August 30, 1973, Chairman MacDonald got the tribal council to pass a resolution authorizing him to enter into negotiations with Exxon and reach an agreement with the company to authorize the development of underlying uranium, fissionable raw materials, and associated minerals. For the next four months, MacDonald and his attorney George Vlassis negotiated with Exxon and reached an agreement authorizing the company to explore for and mine uranium and fissionable or associated raw materials and minerals. Then on January 11, 1974, Mac got the advisory committee to pass a resolution recommending the council pass their resolution to authorize

and direct the chairman to execute the negotiated uranium exploration permit and mining agreement with Exxon. A couple of weeks
later, on January 24, MacDonald got the tribal council to pass a
resolution authorizing and directing him as chairman to execute
the negotiated permit and agreement with the company for and on
behalf of the Navajo Nation. The resolution further authorized Mac
as chairman to do all things necessary or appropriate to implement
the permit and agreement. The resolution was classified as a "Class
C" Resolution meaning "No BIA Action Required."

In terms of dynamic power relationships, the tribal council
wasn't a BIA puppet anymore. It was now an Exxon puppet.

Then things got really obscured after January 24. The BIA
didn't do anything about the tribally approved lease—not that it was
supposed to if the colonial agency was to honor the tribe's Class C
Resolution requirement. However, the BIA-decolonized tribe didn't
do anything either. Even though MacDonald was resolutely authorized and directed by the council's resolution that he signed, he did
not unilaterally execute and implement the permit and agreement.
Finally, months later, the tribal legal department said that "the BIA
must ultimately authorize the lease agreement and this they have, as
yet, not done." MacDonald and Exxon obviously didn't get the BIA
action requirement waiver to get out of the EIS process. Are they
now going to demand a straight NEPA waiver?

There was a corporate school of thought out there that
NEPA didn't apply to Indian tribal lands anyway. It applied to the
non-Indian public domain (such as BLM lands), but Indian lands
were "private lands," not public lands. So, if there was no NEPA
requirement on Indian lands, then there was no EIS requirement.
Another industry school of thought was that NEPA (and its EIS
requirement) didn't apply to Indian lands if there was not a major
federal action involved in the project approval and implementation process. This was based on the deliberate misinterpretation of
the statute that secretarial approval of a lease does not constitute a
major federal action because the secretary was not a project sponsor or in charge of a sponsoring agency, for instance, the Bureau of

Reclamation proposing a right-of-way to string a bunch of power-lines from the Navajo Power Plant to the Central Arizona Project.

There is another pro-development school of thought—this one is pretty dangerous—that acknowledged that NEPA applied to non-Indian projects on Indian lands, but doing an EIS isn't necessary if the initial assessment (however inadequately done) of the environmental impacts of the proposed action were found to be insignificant. This was the enemy's preferred alternative—minimize the severity of the anticipated impacts on paper so they appeared insignificant and minor. But with Exxon (even before the Exxon Valdez incident), it was all about a megaproject that would literally turn the entire northern portion of the Navajo Nation into a permanent radioactive and toxic wasteland. Uranium extraction and processing is not a benign activity. It is a violent technology. Its impacts are violent. It kills. It kills on a horrific scale. Even though the Navajo tribal government was an Exxon puppet, why would it not want an environmental impact statement to at least consider the significant effects of their partially-approved uranium project on the lives and future of its citizens? Have they no conscience? How could a government be so cruel to its own people?

———

While I was doing library research on the Exxon uranium issue, Fred was mobilizing the masses in the actual lease area. As an affected Shiprock resident, he knew about the danger of radiation exposure. His family home was right across the highway from the abandoned KMC-VCA uranium mill and unremediated tailings disposal site. Just south of old mill road was the Fairchild Corporation electronics assembly plant that also presented a growing radioactive hazard.

Most of the Shiprock chapter lands were located within the Exxon lease. The uranium lease also covered most of the Red Rock, Sanostee, Two Grey Hills, and Beclabito chapter lands. The residents of these five chapters have had bad experiences with past uranium development and didn't want any more. Leading the Navajo uranium resistance, Fred secured resolutions from the five-chapter area unanimously opposing Exxon's proposed uranium exploration, mining, and milling project in their backyard. But the heartless tribal government in Window Rock ignored their resolutions and approved the lease on January 24, 1974.

I later met with Fred Johnson and Al Henderson at UNM to discuss the TG&E and Exxon issues. Al was working with Phil Reno at the NCC branch in Shiprock. Al's aunt Mary and her family live at Table Mesa, located within the Exxon uranium lease.

———

Several weeks after our meeting, Farmington happened and we were diverted.

However, the diversion created some unexpected opportunities for the uranium opposition. At the second march, I ran into Leonard Watchman and his uncle Leo, who had recently announced his candidacy for Navajo tribal chairman. We talked about tribal political issues, including the less-than-legal Exxon uranium lease (which was incumbent Chairman MacDonald's baby). Well, one thing led to another, and after the march, Leo became a plaintiff in a lawsuit to force the BIA to comply with NEPA and conduct necessary draft and final environmental impact statements for the tribally approved but not yet federally approved Exxon lease. The suit was eventually successful (though Uncle Leo's run for tribal chairman was not).

There were also other changes during that long, hot summer. Fred resigned as DNA People's Legal Services deputy director to work with CNL as a full-time volunteer. He also took much of his continuing legal advocacy work on the TG&E and Exxon issues with him. He was still a licensed Navajo tribal court advocate and retained extensive ties within the legal community. Al was in the process of moving from Shiprock to Albuquerque but operated effectively from his transitional Shiprock and ABQ bases. Like Fred, Al continued to work on the TG&E and Exxon issues. I was based at EOC in Farmington during the late spring and summer.

In August, Fred announced that he was running for a seat in the Navajo tribal council as the Shiprock delegate. Al and I resumed our academic studies at UNM.

———

Then, in early September, NIYC happened and I was diverted again. But not for long.

Two months later, a Karen Silkwood called the office wanting to talk to somebody about what Kerr-McGee was doing at a uranium-nuclear facility where she was working in Oklahoma. Gerry and I were out of town (Gerry was on the east coast and I was meeting with Phil Loretto and Art Neskahi regarding a hate crime committed against a young Navajo man at the College Inn in Durango). At the time, I didn't know very much about the nuclear fuel cycle (as it was called then). I thought that after the uranium was mined and milled, it was sent directly to a nuclear power plant—like the way mined and processed coal was directly sent to an electrical generating station. I didn't know there were other stages involved, such as uranium conversion, enrichment, and fabrication before the fissionable product was finally used to produce nuclear energy and that there were separate but related facilities for each of those stages.

Karen worked at the Cimarron Fuel Fabrication Plant near Crescent, Oklahoma. She and her trade union were working on documenting and exposing serious health and safety regulation violations at the plant. The union also charged that the highest doses of radiation exposure in the nuclear fuel chain occurred "at the point of production." I think one of the things Karen wanted to talk to us about was the occupational connection between worker health and safety issues at the uranium mines and mills on and near Navajo and Pueblo lands in the Southwest and similar concerns at the uranium nuclear facilities in Oklahoma—particularly the corporate link between Kerr-McGee's abandoned and unreclaimed uranium mines and the unremediated mill tailings storage sites in Northern Navajo and KM's uranium conversion and fabrication plants near Crescent and Gore in Oklahoma. The Gore facility was located on Cherokee lands. At that time, eighteen Navajo former uranium miners in the Red Rock-Cove area had died of lung cancer and many more were dying. A number of Navajo former uranium millers were also dying of silicosis.

Karen Silkwood never called back. Several days after Gerry and I returned, we heard that Karen had died in a mysterious car accident in the course of her brave advocacy work for radiation victims. Following an independent investigation of the suspicious circumstances surrounding her untimely death, most union organizers and anti-nuclear activists believed that she was intentionally targeted, set up, and assassinated by Kerr-McGee's "death squad."

In the meantime, Kerr-McGee was expanding its uranium leaseholdings in the Grants Mineral Belt that extended from Church Rock to Cañoncito. The regional uranium mineral belt—approximately 120 miles long and 30 miles wide—underlay Eastern Navajo, Far Eastern Navajo (Cañoncito), Acoma Pueblo, and Laguna Pueblo lands. During the uranium boom in the southern San Juan Basin from 1971 to 1979, KM became the nation's largest uranium leaseholder. The company operated eight uranium mines in the Church Rock and Ambrosia Lake areas of the Grants Uranium Belt. It also operated the nation's largest uranium mill at Ambrosia Lake.

Exxon was also a major uranium leaseholder during the seventies, but the company's 400,000-acre uranium leasehold at Navajo in the northern San Juan Basin was having problems. Leo Watchman's successful NEPA lawsuit had the desired effect of significantly delaying the proposed federal approval of the Exxon lease. Soon, the Public Service Company of New Mexico withdrew its plans to build a uranium-based nuclear power plant on BLM exchange lands at Bisti. The company did, however, proceed with its plans to build a coal-fired electrical generating station at the Bisti site.

In early January 1976, Navajo tribal councilmen Fred Johnson and Don Noble died in a mysterious small airplane crash near the uranium boomtown of Grants, the Uranium Capital of the World. It was located in the center of the Grants Mineral Belt—the largest uranium exploration and production region in the nation. At the time of their tragic deaths, Fred and Don were returning to Window Rock after an extremely frustrating meeting with BIA Commissioner Morris Thompson and Interior Secretary Thomas Kleppe in Washington, DC. Thompson and Kleppe were the lead defendants in Leo Watchman's case. Fred and Don fiercely debated the legality or illegality of the pending Exxon uranium lease, which contained thirteen federal Indian leasing regulation waivers. One stipulation in the lease included waiving the right of the tribe, as landlord or lessor, to cancel the lease if the company, as tenant or lessee, violated the contract's terms and conditions (some joint venture!). Suffice to say Thompson and Kleppe fully supported the highly unconscionable, if not illegal, waivers.

After the deaths of Fred and Don, I felt that I should become more active in Navajo and Indian uranium and nuclear issues.

———

In early April, I went deep into the belly of the beast and testified in total opposition to the Rape of Mount Taylor and the violent pillaging of other sacred Indian lands in the Grants Mineral Belt at a public hearing held by the rabidly pro-uranium New Mexico Legislative Energy Committee in Grants.

> Gulf Oil Company is developing the nation's largest under-ground uranium mine at the base of the Turquoise Mountain. Grants is projected to become the second-largest city in the State of New Mexico. Industrial armies are marching, and lines of outposts are positioned along the mineral-driven Tiguex-Cibola Trail. A widening swath of destruction and desecration follows the latest wave of New Men invaders across ancient holy land that stretches from the red rock cathedrals of Church Rock to the sentinel volcanic necks of Cañoncito. On both sides of the Continental Divide, the spine of Grandmother Dinétah, a new drilling rig, then a mine, and then a mill pops up every twenty-four hours, seven days a week. Generating and then distributing piles of radioactive mine wastes and mill tailings like smallpox blankets

dropped on targeted tribal populations on an area-specific
basis, the technological monster, the death that creeps upon
the earth, continues its advance through the regional uranium belt, leaving extinction-based contamination in its
wake. The situation is absolute. In order for our children
to live, the monster must die. We, the Human Beings, must
slay the monster.

After delivering my testimony to the shocked committee, I was
immediately approached by attorney Barry Levine of DNA People's
Legal Services, economist Eric Natwig of the Navajo Tribal Office
of Program Development, Superintendent Bobby Eason of the
BIA Eastern Navajo Agency, director Sally Rodgers of the Central
Clearinghouse (who also used to work with Tom Campbell), and
reporter Sherry Robinson of the Grants-Milan *Uranium Empire
Reporter*. They all wanted copies of my full statement.

Barry had presented testimony on the legal history of the
uranium-rich Eastern Navajo reservation extension. He stated that
the 1.9-million-acre extension was illegally disestablished. The
original executive ordered and established, congressionally confirmed, reservation extension boundary "must extend eastward fifty
miles" from the present boundary. He also stated that the "mineral
rights in much of the area may need to be revested to the tribe with
reparation of all past rents and royalties." The minerals in the legally
established exterior boundaries included coal, uranium, oil, and
gas. Eric testified that unmitigated social impacts and unbudgeted
economic costs of an unmanageable uranium boom in the Eastern
Navajo Agency would quickly overwhelm the capacity of the existing infrastructure at Church Rock and Crownpoint. Bobby sent me
an excellent overview of current and projected uranium exploration, mining, and milling projects in the checkerboard, split-estate,
and multi-jurisdictional lands of the Eastern Agency. Sally was
monitoring the development of the United Nuclear Corporation
uranium mill at Church Rock. Sherry interviewed me and later
wrote a supportive article on our testimony at the hearing.

A week later, I was invited to speak at a public meeting at the Crownpoint chapterhouse concerning a large uranium mine project that Continental Oil Company was planning to build near the community. I couldn't go to the meeting because I had to be at the office that week to deal with the usual tsunami of office management and challenges. The never-ending conflict between my administrative work and my organizing work was killing me. I asked Herb Blatchford and Marley Shebala to go in my stead. Herb knew the uranium issue well and was an excellent speaker in the Navajo language. I asked Marley, from the Kiva Club, to join him because her mother Vivian and her daughter Gina were living in the uranium-impacted community of Crownpoint. From all reports, they were exemplary as an elder-youth team at the meeting. Sherry Robinson also covered the all-day meeting for the weekly *Uranium Empire Reporter*.

NIYC opened and briefly operated a field office in Crownpoint to monitor uranium activity in the Eastern Navajo Agency. However, finding and then keeping the right person to staff the office was a problem we could not overcome. When things didn't work out in Crownpoint, we considered opening an NIYC field office in Grants to track uranium leasing and development in the Grants Mineral Belt. The same set of problematic personnel issues arose, so we reconsidered and did not pursue the Grants field office option.

After a while, this cat named Kent Ware started coming around the office and asking me and Gerry about what NIYC was going to do on the Mount Taylor issue. We were a little wary of Kent (not because his last name was Ware) because he was representing Gulf Oil Company that was digging the nation's deepest underground uranium mine shafts into Mount Taylor. He was a Kiowa and an attorney but was working for the enemy. Gulf sent him to find out what our strategy was to protect the sacred mountain under attack. Herb later told us that Kent Ware was a corporate scout—a modern professional Indian scout for the advancing, encircling corporate cavalry of Gulf. This was the same Gulf that was flaying the skin of Mother Earth with its brutal coal strip mining operations outside of Window Rock. The same Gulf that was a major state and federal leaseholder in the Bisti-Star Lake coal development region. The same Gulf that was invading Mariano Lake—even as we spoke. In sum, Herb said that Kent Ware was not a good man and advised us not to have a relationship with him. That way, he'll go away. So, we stopped talking to Kent and, after a while, he went away. What would we do without Herb. . . .

In August, I testified at the Exxon draft environmental impact statement (DEIS) hearing in Window Rock. The DEIS was woefully inadequate and only written to justify the bad Exxon lease. It was clear that Exxon and MacDonald had gotten to the BIA's central office and they were all in it together. We faced an uphill battle. Three months later, the Exxon final environmental impact statement was issued. It was still inadequate but that didn't stop them. They were on a fast track.

In January 1977, Secretary of Interior Thomas Kleppe approved the Exxon uranium lease with the aforementioned waivers. DNA People's Legal Services and NIYC filed a lawsuit representing seventeen Navajo plaintiffs from the lease area against Interior Secretary Kleppe et al. in the US District Court in Albuquerque. We charged that the final EIS for the lease was grossly inadequate and violated the intent and letter of the National Environmental Policy Act. Al Henderson's aunt Mary was one of the plaintiffs in the suit.

Ruling against the plaintiffs, the federal district court dismissed our lawsuit. We appealed the unjust ruling to the US Court of Appeals in Denver, but our appeal was denied—not on the basis of substantive facts and law—but on the defendants' meritless arguments, which were fraught with distortion and frivolous technicalities. Muttering it was a conspiracy, Herb suggested that we sue the court system for obstruction of justice.

With its lease boundaries secured and patrolled by corporate border guards, Exxon arrogantly asserted its superior property rights (thanks to the waivers) of entry to and development of mineable and millable uranium, fissionable raw materials, and associated minerals within its 625-square mile surface and subsurface estate.

The lease exploration stage would last six years. Preliminary drilling indicated sufficient reserves to supply four mines and two mills. The mines and mills were planned to be built during the lease development stage.

There were still no laws to compensate radiation victims and survivors of past uranium development. There were no laws to reclaim and remediate abandoned uranium mines and mills. There was no governmental or corporate responsibility to address these heinous environmental crimes. With the renewed uranium rush, our tribal homelands were being invaded or reinvaded by outsiders. It was a foreign invasion or reinvasion. Land was being taken. People were dying. These are the elements of war. The Indian Wars were not yet over.

In June, Karla Naha (Hopi) called and said that she wanted to meet with me in private. Karla had been an excellent legal secretary for us but had since moved on. She was working for the BIA in Flagstaff and had moved back to Albuquerque, so I drove downtown and picked her up for lunch at La Hacienda in Old Town. We talked over a couple of Fire Eater Specials and a pitcher of iced tea. She was now working in a special BIA office dealing with uranium matters. She said the office was in charge of the new San Juan Regional Uranium Study Program, which was analyzing the benefits and costs of increased uranium leasing and development on Indian lands in the San Juan Basin (including the Grants Mineral Belt). She shared some pretty frightful statistics that included a recent projection that there would be 107 uranium mines and twenty-one uranium mills operating on or near Indian lands in the San Juan Basin by 2000. That was more than triple the number of currently operating uranium extraction and processing facilities in the basin. That was madness, I told her. The regional and cumulative impacts and costs of the projected high development scenario and associated boomtown syndrome effects would surely wipe out the tribes and pueblos in the directly affected area. The ministers of genocide had it all planned out. In radioactive terms, we were already being nuked. And now they are preparing to escalate their nuclear war against us and our unborn. Our lunch meeting was brief, but we agreed to stay in regular contact.

In August, Elouise Chicharello asked me to serve as an adviser and resource person for the UNM American Indian History Project (AIHP) that she was co-coordinating with Diane Reyna (Taos Pueblo). They, along with Louise Linkin (Navajo) and Christine Zuni (Isleta Pueblo), were working on a film project on uranium. They were also working with Rich Nafziger of the Albuquerque-based Americans for Indian Opportunity (AIO), who was writing an AIO Red Paper on uranium. Fellow AIHP adviser Junella Haynes set up a meeting between Rich and me at Baca's. The meeting led to another meeting at Jack's.

In fact, it was at Jack's where I had an earlier issue-related meeting with the new NIYC paralegal, Aldine Farrier, who told me about the tribal uranium experience on her Spokane reservation in Washington. Then Grey Cutler of our youth recreation program told me about the Eastern Shoshone-Northern Arapaho uranium experience on his joint reservation in Wyoming. And then new NIYC investigative researcher Jene Hood told me that she and her daughter Daisy had just moved from the Ute Mountain Ute reservation where Mobil Oil Corporation recently leased over 160,000 acres of tribal reservation lands for uranium exploration and development. Following Jene was another investigative researcher, Frank Carrillo (Laguna Pueblo), who shared his pueblo's uranium experience with the still-expanding Jackpile Mine. Then, organization investigative researcher Geneva Thompson from Cañoncito informed me in late December that Exxon was planning to lease the entire Cañoncito Navajo reservation for uranium drilling and mining.

That did it!

———

For the next three years, my main organizing work focused on uranium and nuclear issues in Indian Country: Four Corners, San Juan Basin, Grants Mineral Belt, Middle Rio Grande, Black Hills, Great

Basin, Intermountain, Great Lakes, Grand Canyon, and Colorado Plateau. Most of the major stuff from 1978 to 1980 is in my papers.

By early 1981, the once-advancing uranium and nuclear industry were in full retreat. The boom in the Grants Mineral Belt and San Juan Uranium Basin had busted. Even Exxon was withdrawing from the Four Corners area.

But we had little time to celebrate as we faced myriad challenges on old and new fronts.

CHAPTER 6

THE CORRUPTION OF TRIBAL GOVERNMENT

In August 1972, I met with Mitch Fowler and Iva Palucci in Gallup to discuss the progressive work of the Navajos for a Better Tribal Government, of which they were both founding members. They and other members of the reservation-based organization had recently demonstrated outside the Window Rock Motor Inn, where the non-Indian chaired Navajo Tribal Coal Gasification Task Force was meeting behind closed doors with representatives of the coal gasification companies hoping to construct and operate large mine-mouth coal gasification plants on the Navajo reservation. One of the members of the new tribal government reform advocacy group, Larry Casuse, was also working with SID and IAE. Larry was everywhere that summer.

Mitch said they were protesting the lack of transparency and accountability in the conduct of official tribal business and that the recent closed-door meeting with the coal gasification company reps illustrated exactly why tribal citizen action was necessary. As a protester's picket sign read, "No more secret deals." Mitch also said that the Navajo Tribe should have an open meetings law and tribal equivalents of a Federal Register (so we know when they're about to sell out) and a Freedom of Information Act (so we can get copies of leases and contracts). In addition, he said, the tribe should have a natural resources utilization policy (our national policy, not the stranger's corporate policy), alongside other tribal government reform issues that must be addressed. In the meantime, Mitch and Iva said, the Navajos for a Better Tribal Government would serve as a vigilant watchdog for the Navajo public.

It all sounded good, so I told Mitch to count me in as another Navajo for a better tribal government. I knew the central tribal government in Window Rock existed for the principal purpose of facilitating the foreign invaders. There was a history to that, and that history had to do with oil and other reservation resources. In fact, I had read in an oil and gas publication that "the first official report of oil in New Mexico occurred in 1882 when a prospecting party discovered a flowing oil spring in the northwest region of the New Mexico Territory" and that "a U.S. Geological Survey report stated that a band of Navajo Indians drove the workmen away before they could determine the quantity of oil obtainable." What the pro-oil and gas publication did not state was that in 1882, the New Mexico portions of the 1868 Navajo treaty reservation and adjacent 1878 and 1880 executive order reservation additions constituted the northwest area of the so-called New Mexico Territory. The contiguous Navajo tribal lands were occupied and used by Navajo tribal members, so non-tribal trespassers on tribal property were run off by a band of bros. But the invaders were persistent and, in 1902, they somehow got mineral entry to the tribal treaty reservation.

According to part of a statement by John Worth of Sun Company to the US House Committee on Indian Affairs, "Of course, we can go into a treaty reserve. For instance, twenty years ago, I made a treaty with the Navajo Indians for this treaty reserve; we got a blanket lease for the entire thing and we had the right to prospect for minerals but we did not find anything and we threw it up." Worth's testimony was presented in 1922 at a hearing held by the committee on a congressional bill to open Navajo executive order reservation lands to unrestricted oil and gas leasing and development. The bill, drafted and introduced on behalf of the encroaching oil and gas industry, was illegal in content—it did not even contain a provision requiring tribal consent to the proposed leasing and development. Worth's "treaty" and "lease" were clearly illegal, but that did not stop the Pennsylvania oilman from getting full access to the unexplored tribal treaty reservation mineral estate.

Still, there was no way—not by any stretch of the imagination—that he could have made a treaty, much less a lease, with the Navajo Indians because the folks were all spread out on the 3.5-million-acre treaty reservation. They would not have stopped what they were doing and marched obediently to the BIA Indian Agency at Fort Defiance to negotiate with this one white man and give him the tribal key to the treaty rez. Furthermore, Indian treaty-making was outlawed by the federal government in 1871. The Navajo Tribe of Indians never, ever, made a treaty with a non-governmental entity, much less an individual. What probably happened was that Worth approached a corrupt BIA Indian agent, waved a twenty-dollar bill, and got what he wanted in terms of private ingress and egress to the unquantified mineral estate of the tribal treaty reservation. When Worth said he didn't find anything, that should have put an end to ever seeing him or his kind ever again. Well, not exactly.

It wasn't long—less than twenty years—before oil was discovered on treaty reservation lands by the Midwest Refining Company. Secretary of the Interior Albert Fall (of Teapot Dome Scandal infamy) set up a puppet tribal government to give Midwest, Sun, and the other corporate invaders all the mineral leases they wanted. It went downhill from there. Fifty years of exploitation later, I'm here meeting with Mitch and Iva about how to turn things around and make them better politically. We had to do something. Polity-wise, it couldn't get much worse.

———

In the summer of 1970, then-Navajo chairman candidate Peter MacDonald spoke at Gap, saying that he was not opposed to outside development per se, but wanted power over how the arrangement was brought in. His campaign statement lacked specifics but sounded pretty good at the time. Then, after he became chairman, he said that he wasn't necessarily opposed to strip mining. I interpreted that to mean he wasn't unconditionally opposed to the continuing Rape of Black Mesa or to the violent strip mining at Nenahnezad and Black Hat. He did, however, say that he opposed the low lease rentals and royalties the tribe was getting from the strip miners. So, I guess in Chairman MacDonald's mind, it would be alright for Peabody to continue to strip mine our sacred mountain as long as the tribe got a good money deal out of it. Of course, the money—as all the grassroots know—would just go into some politician's pocket or disappear into that black hole in Window Rock, with none of it trickling down to the hogan level. No wonder the impoverished masses called him Peter MacDollar.

The tribal power elite leasing away our holy mountain for thirty pieces of silver was not economic justice, the mining was not environmental justice, and the mining-related relocation was not social justice. I also found no evidence of political justice at Black Mesa and now Burnham. It was bad enough that the chairman's non-Navajo-chaired Navajo Tribal Coal Gasification Task Force was meeting behind closed doors with the coal gasification company representatives; these guys hadn't even gone out to the Burnham chapter to inform, much less consult with, the people who actually lived on the land where the coal gas plants were going to be built. The tribe always complained about how the BIA never consulted them on important matters of tribal concern. Yet, they were doing the same thing—not consulting with their own people on the planned coal gasification development. It looked like what had happened at Black Mesa was going to happen at Burnham and, again, without the consent of the very people who resided on the land. That wasn't right.

Three months earlier, El Paso Natural Gas Company had flown a group of tribal officials to its corporate headquarters in El Paso for a two-day briefing on its proposed coal gasification project. All expenses were paid by the company, including the use of its charter airplanes. According to the briefing agenda, the first item was a "social and get-acquainted meeting" with company representatives. However, we heard—through credible whispers at Henry's Corner in Fort Defiance—that the tribal delegates just got drunk and somebody brought out the "cuchi-cuchi girls." We also heard that some of the delegates later ended up across the border in Juarez to see the "donkey show." The details of the rest of the two-day briefing session were sketchy, but we could only imagine. It was even rumored that one of the honorable tribal delegates missed the return charter jet flight and had to take the bus back. Factual or not, it was still disturbing to learn that the off-reservation meeting was held hundreds of miles away from the uninformed and unconsulted Burnham chapter.

———

Mitch was always talking about loss of land and loss of control of land. Historically, he said, tribal councils were created by the enemy to take our land or take control of our land. The first tribal council was created by the Army at Fort Sumner to sign the land cession Treaty of 1868 that ceded 90 percent of our aboriginal homeland. After the treaty was signed, the tribal council was unilaterally disbanded. The treaty also contained a provision that authorized the cession of the rest of our land. The Secretary of Interior later created another tribal council to sign leases with oil and gas companies. These leases were actually cessions of land and resources to the companies, often ninety-nine-year leases or for as long as the lease resources were produced in paying quantities. In any case, the people who lived on the land lost control to the alien invaders.

The People were losing or had lost control of seventy-one thousand acres of prime grazing lands along the Chaco River to energy resource development. Thirty-one thousand acres of productive rangeland were given to Utah International, Inc. and possibly Western Gasification Company. Forty thousand grazing acres were ceded to El Paso Natural Gas Company and Consolidation Coal Company. According to the prestigious National Academy of Sciences, the seventy-one thousand acres of leased-and-lost pastureland was already written off as a national sacrifice area because of its low or non-existent reclamation potential. At that time, there was no federal Surface Mining Control and Reclamation Act due to strong congressional lobbying by the powerful mining industry. The seventy-one thousand acres of Navajo pastoral range were to be taken out of grazing resource production, condemned to be strip-mined and destroyed forever.

———

One time, Mitch and I took a road trip from Tuba City to Torreon and kept picking up hitchhikers along the way. Outside of Tuba, Mitch said the Navajo political economy was dependent on outside capital investment. I agreed, saying that it was—in a larger sense— an outgrowth of American invasion, conquest, colonization, and exploitation. After stopping at Keams Canyon for gas, we picked up hitchhiker number one, who turned out to be an anarchist. Between Keams and Steamboat Canyon, he said that he thought the Treaty of 1868 was a surrender document and that the Navajo chiefs who signed it were all sellouts. We then picked up hitchhiker number two at the Summit. He said that it was stupid to criticize the tribal government while ignoring the powerful outside forces that control and manipulate it. We then dropped off hitchhiker number one at Fedmart in Window Rock and picked up hitchhiker number three and his dog. He thought that we should support the tribal government when they do good and oppose them when they do bad. His owner agreed. After dropping off hitchhiker number two at JB Tanners, we drove north and then turned east, south of Tohatchi. The tribal cops stopped us at Standing Rock and made Mitch open the trunk to make sure that we weren't bootleggers headed to the squaw dance at Borrego Pass. Dropping off hitchhiker number three and his dog at KFC in Crownpoint, we motored north and then turned east, south of Becenti. At Milepost 76, we picked up hitchhiker number four, who was waving a dollar bill. Coincidently, he was the mad uncle of hitchhiker number one. Number four opined that the bastard tribal government was an extension of the federal-corporate state of Amerika. We gratefully accepted his dollar bill for gas and dropped him off at his ex-wife's place in Torreon before turning around and returning to Tuba City. Over late-night coffee, chile beans and fry bread at the Navajo-Hopi Kitchen, we evaluated our road trip and planned another one from Aneth to Ramah. The discourse proved to be quite instructive in our sweeping survey of the tribal body politic.

After the Thanksgiving Day march and demonstration, there was a rumor going around that I had wanted the protesters to take over the BIA area office in Gallup as a continuation of the protest. The rumor was probably planted by a frustrated agent provocateur or operative in our midst. Anyway, Mitch Fowler and Penny Hunter met with me in Farmington in December and asked if the rumor was true. I told them it wasn't but added that I did support the AIM-led November takeover of the BIA's central office in Washington, DC.

Mitch had recently had his day in court on the Thanksgiving Day confrontation with the state police. The case was now behind him, and he wanted to turn to direct action against the tribe. He had been talking to other people in our group about a takeover of Chairman MacDonald's office and some of them seemed up for it. He then asked, "what about you?" I replied, "I'm ready when they are." He then asked me to write up some demands for us to negotiate during our occupation. I did and then we got together for a major planning meeting in Gallup, but it did not go as planned because only Mitch, me, and another fellow showed up. Clearly, most of the rest of the group were not yet ready for direct action. We decided to wait until they were ready. Then, we would make our move.

From January to May 1973, the Navajos for a Better Tribal Government evolved into the Diné Coalition. I didn't have anything to do with the evolution or transition process—that happened under the brilliant leadership of Mitch Fowler. When it came to progressive organizational development and coalition building, he was a genius.

Later in June, I (as IAE coordinator) assisted Shirley Martin of SID when she coordinated a dignified, effective student demonstration in front of the Navajo tribal council chambers. The peaceful and legal demonstration put long overdue public attention on the critical need to empower and enfranchise Navajo youth as tribal citizens and future leaders of the Diné Nation.

I also helped Shirley when she coordinated the first and second annual Navajo Nation Youth Conferences in 1973 and 1974. A call was issued to the participants at the plenary session of the 1974 conference to directly address the current crisis of confidence in the Navajo tribal government. The call came in the form of a strongly worded resolution that Shirley had asked me to write. I was truly honored and blessed to be part of this growing reservation-wide tribal youth movement.

A Tohatchi native, Shirley also worked with the IAE TG&E Project group and the Tohatchi-based TG&E Investigation Committee that fought against the then-proposed TG&E powerline project. She believed that the right-of-way agents of the Navajo Tribal Office of Land Administration had conspired with the Tucson Gas and Electric Company to illegally obtain easements from Navajo land users through fear, intimidation, and blackmail tactics. The blatant use of such tactics, she felt, formed a wanton pattern of flagrant violations of tribal citizens' and reservation residents' federal civil rights.

In the summer of 1973, Shirley also worked on the US Civil Rights Commission's three days of public hearings in Window Rock. At the hearings in October, she testified on the continuing violations of Navajo civil rights on the colonized and exploited reservation. Based on the power and force of her testimony and others, the Commission later issued its historic report entitled "The Navajo Nation: An American Colony."

Shirley Martin, only in her late teens, was a bright star in the movement and my work with her in 1973 and 1974 formed a very special period in my life that I will always cherish.

———

I also spent quite a bit of time with Fred Johnson in the summer of 1974. After he resigned from DNA to join CNL, he stayed at my

New Moon trailer in Farmington for a while and, in the evenings, we would talk for hours—sometimes all night—about Navajo and Indian political issues, particularly tribal government corruption in Window Rock and on the Pine Ridge Sioux reservation (the liberation of Wounded Knee had a lot to do with corrupt tribal leadership). We agreed that Peter MacDonald was a slick version of Dickie "Goon Squad" Wilson, the corrupt tribal chairman at Pine Ridge. We also agreed that MacDonald's sophisticated image would lead to his longevity in office, which didn't bode well for the likelihood of clean tribal government any time soon.

Fred later moved back to Shiprock and announced his candidacy to run for the Navajo tribal council. I would like to think that our long conversations under the stars in Totah had something to do with his personal decision to seek the position of Shiprock council delegate. His successful campaign was based on fundamental tribal political reform.

———

In January 1975, I began working with Fred, the new councilman, on the coal gasification and the closely related AFL-CIO issues. As part of his coal and uranium development agenda, the re-elected Tribal Chairman MacDonald supported opening the reservation to Big Labor. Several years earlier, he had gotten the tribal council to pass a pro-labor union resolution authorizing him as chairman "to do any and all things necessary, incidental or advisable, to accomplish the purpose of this resolution." In his first term, MacDonald developed a political relationship with the AFL-CIO that helped him get re-elected in November 1974.

Shortly after the inauguration of his second four-year term, he signed an agreement with the AFL-CIO Building Trades Council to unionize the energy-rich reservation. The presidents of fourteen labor unions also signed the agreement. The AFL-CIO wanted to take over and control major construction projects on and near the reservation and contract tribal manpower funds from the Navajo DOL and CETA to train tribal human resources for employment at the planned coal gas plants and uranium mines and mills. The union hoped to subsidize the 'special needs' of Big Labor's national presence in DC or, as Navajo Nancy at Navajo Community College put it, "to pay for Jimmy Hoffa's whorehouses." It didn't look good. Big Industry wanted to take over and control the rest of our remaining coal and uranium resources. Now, Big Labor wanted to take over and control our human resources. The worst part was that MacDonald was making it happen.

Fortunately, we now had Fred Johnson in the seventy-four-member council to challenge MacDonald's "one-man rule." Other strong council delegates—Lewis Etsitty, Don Noble, Dr. Annie Wauneka, Raymond Smith (who was one of JoAllan's great-uncles), Willis Peterson, and Wilson Halona—opposed MacDonald's unilateral policies. These powerful tribal legislators, especially Dr. Wauneka, had considerable influence over other council members. We had the potential to even things up on the council floor on certain issues. I say "we" because Fred included me in their caucuses. We would meet as a group at the Window Rock Lodge or Motor Inn when the council was in session to develop a legislative strategy to thwart MacDonald's pro-development agenda that we viewed as definitely not in the Navajo public interest. Frankly, we could not see how more colonialism, imperialism, and exploitation could ever be in the tribal public interest.

We had the numbers to effectively counter one of MacDonald's reckless coal gas initiatives during the spring session. But the chairman was clever and efficiently worked the advisory committee—his advisory committee—for what he could get when the full council was not in session. Plus, his white-led coal gas task force was apparently still doing its thing with the prospective coal gassers. It was hard to tell when or where they were meeting because even our most trusted and reliable information cells and mole networks in the tribal capital didn't know. The super secrecy surrounding the coal gas negotiations was disturbing.

The labor unions were some pretty rough boys. At an April meeting in Farmington, Harris and Claudeen Arthur, Phil Reno, and I met Northern Cheyenne tribal leaders Edwin Dahl and Bob Bailey, who told us about the problems their tribe was having with the unions on and near their reservation. Fred later visited the coal-rich Northern Cheyenne reservation in Montana and confirmed that "they are in hot water with the unions. The unions are controlling their tribal council. When you agree to the unions, then almost automatically what goes with it is the deterioration of tribal sovereignty."

The Navajo tribal council "delayed approval" of the agreement co-signed by MacDonald and the AFL-CIO "until further word could be received regarding the wishes of the Navajo people." Although the chairman had signed the agreement on behalf of the Navajo Tribe, the council—the official governing body of the Navajo Nation—had not approved it. The council also did not approve a related agreement known as the AFL-CIO HRDI Manpower Training Project that was also co-signed by MacDonald and the AFL-CIO.

The tribal council then established a committee, with Don Noble as chairman, to investigate the legality of the agreement and contract. The Fort Defiance Agency Council also unanimously passed a resolution opposing the agreement and contract and requesting the tribal council disapprove the legally questionable documents. Don Noble, the Fort Defiance Agency Council chairman, met with AFL-CIO Building Trades Council president Robert Georgine and MacDonald's attorney George Vlassis at the national union headquarters in DC. According to Don, MacDonald and Vlassis "have been dealing, talking, signing agreements before the tribal council even knew what was happening. Everything was done under wraps, causing us to become suspicious. Our feeling was, and is still, if everything is on the up and up, why wasn't everything in the open? Today, the majority of our people are asking, 'what is all of this business with the Unions?'"

Don's two-day meeting with Georgine and George yielded no direct answers. At the end of day two, the tedious drone of their vague and evasive responses to his crisp, concise questioning became just noise. They weren't going to tell him anything—not really. On his long flight back, he had a window seat and looking down at the smog-choked Pittsburgh it became increasingly clear what they were trying to hide. It was pretty bad too. Don was in a reflective and expansive mood as he, Fred, Herb Blatchford, and I sat in the lobby of the old Hotel Shiprock. He said that he had given this whole union issue a lot of thought since the meeting in DC and wanted to add more context to the next stage of our work.

The young councilman from Ganado had a theory on the enemy, which he shared in shocking detail with us:

> The reservation is too thinly populated to merit even a fraction of the interest shown by the unions, who supported MacDonald's election last year and have turned their lobbying efforts for his benefit. It is strange that Big Labor should accord the sheep-raising reservation giant industrial status. Navajo Nation has fewer people than one-half of Albuquerque and few jobs. . . . There are three parts to a bigger puzzle, and three cooperating elements in the big rip-off of the Navajo Nation. Each puts in their special abilities, each takes out a reward. They are MacDonald, the unions, and the energy development companies. MacDonald signs agreements 'for the Navajo Nation' giving the AFL-CIO complete control of all construction and activity that may lead to construction on or near the sixteen-million-acre Navajo reservation. He also signs contracts sub-granting to the AFL-CIO portions of manpower training funds provided by the Department of Labor to train Navajos. Over twenty-five million federal dollars have been granted recently. The fat contracts allow the AFL-CIO to use the funds to pay part of their staff in the National Office in Washington, and to defray their lobbying expenses. . . . MacDonald then signs mineral lease agreements with big energy development companies (including Exxon for uranium mining, WESCO, a combination of coal gasification interests, El Paso National Gas Company, and others). Contracts have been signed without customary bids. The energy development companies plan to mine, process, transport, and sell the energy products. The unions lobby

Congress and the Interior Department, causing Indian trust protection regulations to be waived and leases to be approved without regulation bids and with lax environmental provisions. The combination, if real would indeed be formidable, and would explain the intensity of the interest shown by Big Labor. . . . They're not suddenly interested in the Navajo reservation because of our jewelry and rugs. MacDonald, the unions, and industry are trying to hold up and shake the Navajo piggy bank. Since the known Navajo coal and uranium reserves are likely to be worth billions of dollars.

There. He laid it all out. There was a lot at stake here.

———

In October and November, we slugged it out with Consolidation Coal Company and El Paso Natural Gas Company. Though we won a major victory on the council floor, we knew—and they knew—they would be back. While we were duking it out with CONPASO in Window Rock, WESCO and the AFL-CIO were busy lobbying in DC for congressional subsidies to the coal gasification industry. Federal coal gas subsidy legislation was introduced in December.

There wasn't much we could do politically on the Exxon uranium lease. MacDonald and the previous tribal council had approved it in early 1974. By late 1975, it was largely a legal matter (although we heard that super-secret lease amendment negotiations were going on in Tucson. MacDonald, Exxon, and the AFL-CIO were pressuring the BIA and Department of Interior to approve the thirteen deadly regulation waivers.)

In early November, the National Congress of American Indians (NCAI) passed a resolution stating that "Indians on and near the reservations have the right to work whether or not members of a union." The resolution further stated that "the National Congress of American Indians notify union organizations, the Department of Labor, and the National Labor Relations Board that it discourages union activity on Indian reservations under the National Labor

Relations Act as inconsistent with Federal Indian Policy and Federal Indian Treaties, Statutes, and Rules and Regulations."

MacDonald was at the NCAI conference in Portland, lobbying against the resolution. Don and Fred were there too, raising important questions for the members of the largest Indian organization to consider why "the chairman (MacDonald) says in one breath that the Navajo Right to Work Law in 1958 makes it illegal for any person to enter into an agreement requiring a person to join a union as a condition of employment but at the same time does not explain why then he executed labor agreements with an organization that does not recognize the Right to Work Law." After the conference, Don and Fred pointed out another major inconsistency, "The chairman also fails to explain why a few years ago, he himself said 'Union organization on the reservation is not consistent with the best interest of the Indian' and now does a complete turnaround. Why has he changed his mind about labor unions on the reservation? Why does he carry the labor unions banner so high when the National Congress of American Indians and most Navajos are opposed to unionization?"

They pointed to another huge inconsistency that involved discrimination against tribal workers on their own reservation. MacDonald's union deal would bring the tribe under the National Labor Relations Act that would favor union hiring preference over Navajo preference and Indian preference—clearly this was not in the interest of full employment on the rez. Finally, they charged that the tribal council was not informed in advance of the chairman's agreement with the AFL-CIO and that without council consent, the agreement was "valueless." Even the independent Navajo Labor Party of Cornfields conceded that the agreement (the HRDI contract) was provisional and should not have been implemented to such an extent until the politics were straightened out, including getting tribal council consent.

It appeared that tribal strongman Peter MacDonald, the AFL-CIO, and the Office of Navajo Labor Relations (now serving as a field office of the national labor union organization) muscled in on the tribal open-shop sector like mobsters.

In mid-November, Navajo tribal council AFL-CIO committee chairman Don Noble reported to the tribal council that his committee had received troubling reports from two contractors on the reservation of recent incidents of "forced recruiting" and "threats" by Office of Navajo Labor Relations director Tom Brose and five AFL-CIO Building Trades Union Council business agents. The contractors reported that the threats made against them by Brose and the boys were "join the union or they would get rough," "join or they would have to tie a knot," and sign up "or else expect many busted pipes." They also reported that the threats of violence "interrupted" two deadline-driven construction projects in the greater Window Rock-St. Michaels growth center corridor. Both Navajo labor-intensive projects were vital to tribal nation-building efforts. The violent threats also had a chilling effect on other essential reservation infrastructure development and improvement projects. According to one longtime political observer, the "reports of threatened violence are expected to strengthen the cause of Navajos who have traditionally endorsed the 'Right to Work.' At present, joining a union is a voluntary choice."

In early December, Annie Wauneka and twelve other council delegates wrote letters to state and federal law enforcement authorities in New Mexico, Arizona, and Colorado requesting "any information you could furnish relating to Mr. (Edward) Urioste and illegal union activities on the Navajo reservation." Urioste was a notorious New Mexico labor union leader who had recently pled guilty in Denver to illegally transporting, shipping, and possessing explosives. After these letters were received, the investigation into Urioste expanded to include a possible connection to the forced, if not violent, unionization of Navajo labor.

Several weeks later, Don Noble finally called for a complete suspension of labor relations between the Navajo Tribe and the AFL-CIO, pending tribal and federal investigations and audits. Don said that Urioste's recent guilty plea to criminal charges and the reported union threats against contractors on the reservation was "sufficient reason as far as this committee is concerned for the Navajo Nation to study very carefully organized labor interventions on the Indian way of life. Organized labor activities such as this smack of labor violence mindful of the (Joseph) Yablonski murders, James Hoffa's disappearance, and a long list of countrywide acts of violence and mayhem that there is no place for on the Navajo reservation." Don continued, "There were charges in November 1974 of organized labor involvement in Navajo tribal elections. This new development so close to the Navajo Nation certainly indicates caution in all Indian dealings with organized labor is warranted."

The developing interests between the parties of the Navajo Tribe and the AFL-CIO regarding future plans for the coal gasification became readily apparent when, in mid-December, "a representative of the union admitted that the agreement would also benefit the unions because of the great amount of construction planned on or near the Navajo reservation in the next few years, especially with the possibility of coal gasification plants now under consideration for the northeastern portion of the reservation."

While outside forces combined to shape the Navajo industrial and labor future, the Indian Self-Determination and Education Assistance Act was passed and signed into law. The BIA publicly supported it and even Commissioner of Indian Affairs Morris Thompson had told the Navajo tribal council that self-determination was a good thing.

However, in December, Commissioner Thompson told BIA Navajo area director Anthony Lincoln to resign from that position and transfer to a newly created but meaningless position in Phoenix—or else. Somebody wanted Tony Lincoln out, and that somebody was Peter MacDonald.

As far as BIA area directors go, Tony wasn't a bad guy—as far as I could tell. First of all, he was a Navajo from the reservation. In fact, he was the first Navajo to be appointed BIA area director for any tribal reservation. The Navajo tribal council passed a resolution supporting the retention of Lincoln as BIA area director and opposing Thompson's transfer order and ultimatum. The council also wrote a letter to Tony directing him not to accept the commissioner's order or any order to any position that would move him out of the Navajo area. The honorable Willis Peterson wrote the letter on behalf of the tribal council. Furthermore, the council resolution was passed in the spirit of self-determination to satisfy the intent of the recently enacted Indian Self-Determination and Education Assistance Act of 1975.

One would think that MacDonald—as chairman of the Navajo tribal council—would support the resolution. After all, in testimony before the Senate Subcommittee on Indian Affairs in Albuquerque on August 29, 1973, MacDonald stated, "First, the area director (at least within the Navajo area office) should be appointed with the advice and consent of the Navajo Tribal Council and serve at their pleasure." Obviously, Tony served at the pleasure of the Navajo tribal council. He certainly did not serve at their displeasure and if he had, then they would have surely passed a resolution to that effect.

There was a lot of speculation regarding the real forces and true pressures pressing for Tony's ouster like, "there have been reports that some of the pressure came from the office of Tribal Chairman Peter MacDonald. There have been other reports that pressure came from important sources in the AFL-CIO, which has been in the process of negotiating a kind of closed shop for itself on the twenty-five-thousand-square-mile Navajo reservation. Has Lincoln done something to stir the ire of the tribal chairman? Or the AFL-CIO?"

Now, it looked like Tony was serving at the displeasure of both MacDonald and the AFL-CIO. What precisely did Tony do to deserve involuntary deportation and exile away from his home reservation? He was not incompetent. He had been the BIA Navajo area director for over four years with no major complaints. Before that, he was Deputy Commissioner of Indian Affairs in DC with no big scandals. These were important positions requiring the proper discharge of trust responsibility based on exacting fiduciary standards. He had to have something on the ball. His job performance at the area and national levels was reportedly outstanding. So, his professionalism was not an issue.

Yet, Commish Thompson, without consulting or even inform-ing the Navajo tribal council, ordered Tony to resign as Navajo area director without cause and to transfer to some Mickey Mouse job in Phoenix without good reason. He gave him just a few days to say yes, or he would have been fired for insubordination. Tony described the new position created for him as a "do nothing" job or an "elephant graveyard." He said, "If you're a supervisor and con-sidered hard to handle, that's where you end up." He had seen that before, where problem supervisors were summarily reassigned by BIA Central to a meaningless or irrelevant position with no author-ity, no responsibility, and no budget. You even have to answer your own phone! The horror, the horror. We heard it's true. There is a special place in BIA hell that is reserved for innovative and renegade supervisors such as him.

Thompson claimed that his sudden personnel action against Tony was routine, saying simply that "from time to time, the commissioner, for the good of the Bureau, makes changes in its policy-making positions." Translation: "Blah, blah, blah." The com-missioner then sent a telegram to the self-determined Navajo tribal council on the bureaucratic disposition of their native son, stating curtly that it would be "inappropriate to discuss the transfer further."

Outraged, Annie Wauneka said that Thompson's telegraphed response to their overwhelming majority resolution was a "slap in the face in light of the Indian Self-Determination Act that was implemented to give the Indians the right of self-government on the reservation." Knowing Annie, she would have liked to have given the disrespectful commissioner a well-deserved slap in the face—like the way she righteously smacked that obnoxious, guffawing Ted Mitchell in the council chambers seven resounding years earlier. Lucky for Thompson, he was two thousand miles away.

Councilman Willis Peterson weighed in, saying that the force of the tribal council resolution on the Lincoln matter overrode Thompson's unilateral action, which unlawfully interfered with the free exercise of the inherent right of self-determination by the nation's largest Indian tribe on the nation's largest Indian reservation. In a letter to Thompson, Fred Johnson wrote that he was "curious as to what happened to the doctrine of Indian self-determination. . . . Is it still law? I would assume by your unprecedented move that the doctrine has been abolished by you alone."

Thompson didn't have an answer. He just kept saying that it was a personnel matter. That was a crock of BS and kind of hard to follow at times. For example, Thompson first gave Tony a deadline of December 24 to accept the transfer order. After news of the controversial order broke, he extended the deadline to January 18, 1976. Something else happened and he moved the deadline back to January 9. And Thompson never mentioned that Tony would be terminated as BIA area director anyway—whether he accepted the transfer or not.

Thompson said that Tony's options were limited to acceptance or rejection of the transfer order. If he rejected it, he could appeal the order to a BIA administrative court. If he rejected it and declined to appeal, then he would be declared AWOL and fired according to civil service rules and regulations. Either way, Tony would be replaced as area director by a yes-man, and the tribe would soon be in a worse situation insofar as self-determination.

Tony, of course, didn't want to resign and transfer. He didn't immediately say yes or no to Thompson's ultimatum; instead, he hired a lawyer to advise him of his personnel rights. "His individual rights? What about our collective right of self-determination," Fred asked. He was frustrated. "Tony Lincolns are a dime a dozen," he said, "What is really important is the *principle* of Indian self-determination. Do we have real self-determination or not? The congressional lawmakers (who legislated the Indian Self-Determination and Education Assistance Act) say we do. That BIA outlaw Morris Thompson says we don't. Well, we'll see about that!" The escalated battle for Navajo self-determination, Fred determined, "generated heated controversy on the Navajo reservation in New Mexico and Arizona, one threatening to equal the magnitude of the Navajo-Hopi land dispute."

Fred had already warned Commissioner Thompson about the possibility of necessary legal action against those—like him—who unwisely go against the law. He also informed the rogue commissioner that he had already written letters to several powerful senators and congressmen requesting their direct political intervention in the Lincoln affair. He then let Thompson know that he had some 'intimate' inside explanation as to why this removal order came about, "but I will withhold revealing it to the public at this time." Thompson was unresponsive—one source said that he didn't know whether to shit or go blind in light of Fred's possession of "intimate" inside information. So, Fred and Don set up a meeting with Thompson's boss, Secretary of Interior Thomas Kleppe, to discuss canceling Thompson's transfer order.

On January 3, 1976, I met with Fred and Don in Shiprock, and they told me about the meeting they were going to have with Kleppe in DC on January 5. They were also planning to meet with Senator Barry Goldwater and other key members of Congress after their meeting with Secretary Kleppe. Don's aunt, Annie Wauneka, had strong connections on Capitol Hill, which they were evidently using. I didn't like Barry Goldwater because he was largely anti-Navajo, but he was also anti-MacDonald and anti-AFL-CIO. Conflicted, I thought, "well, if he can help us on certain issues, I guess that's alright—for now. As long as we don't owe him anything after all this was over." I couldn't see him being our permanent ally.

We also talked some about the "intimate" inside information Fred had and was willing to reveal to the public. He said he had the documents (the contents of which were described as explosive) in his possession but wanted to release them at the right time. Fred said the documents had to do with the AFL-CIO deals, Exxon, coal gasification, and the Navajo-Hopi Land Dispute. The latter threw me for a loop. I had actually supported MacDonald and the AFL-CIO for their strong but ultimately unsuccessful lobbying campaign against the racist land dispute settlement legislation in 1974. I was quite impressed with their directed voter registration and election drive, albeit unsuccessful, against Senator Goldwater, who was behind the anti-Indian legislation that ordered land partition and forced Navajo and Hopi relocation from the partitioned former joint-use area lands. Again conflicted, I just maintained my narrow-minded focus. The situation was complicated enough, and things were not always cut-and-dried. Sometimes, they were gray, even different shades of gray. There was a lot unsaid in those days—especially by me. That's probably why I would brood in my beer so much.

Fred and Don said that Raymond Smith, Willis Peterson, and Wilson Halona would also be part of their delegation to DC. The five Navajo tribal council delegates would formally present the official tribal council resolution opposing Thompson's transfer order. I didn't know it at the time, but *Arizona Republic* investigative journalist Don Bolles was also specially assigned to report on the historic January 5 meeting.

The two-hour meeting with Kleppe did not go well. As reported by Mr. Bolles, Kleppe refused to "reverse his commissioner." In fact, the non-Indian Interior Secretary said that he "must back up his Indian commissioner . . . or else the Bureau of Indian Affairs will be demoralized." Bolles also reported that "Thompson, who sat in on the meeting with several Interior Department aides, insisted the transfer is being sought for the good of the BIA. Kleppe appeared shocked when Johnson said MacDonald was involved in the transfer plot, that it was an internal matter with the Navajos, and that Washington should not be settling it." The meeting reportedly ended with the following exchange.

"Do I understand you are rejecting our plea?" Johnson asked the cabinet officer.

"No," Kleppe replied, "I'll have further action on this after I get a report from the commissioner."

The "further action" and "report" was just BS. They already had their colonial minds made up. Following the meeting, the transfer order still stood and Thompson reissued the long-distance ultimatum to Lincoln. Fred accurately called Thompson an "enemy of the Navajos and all American Indians" and correctly stated that the commissioner "no more believes in self-determination than Adolf Hitler."

In what was known as The Lincoln Conspiracy, a BIA Deep Throat confirmed that MacDonald asked Thompson for Lincoln's ouster in the fall of 1975. He said MacDonald told Thompson that both he, as the chairman, and the tribal council were not satisfied with Lincoln's performance as area director and wanted him ousted and replaced by somebody who would not interfere with tribal government operations. So, thinking that Chairman MacDonald also spoke for the tribal council, Thompson initiated personnel action to terminate Lincoln as area director and transfer him to a specially created but non-essential position in Phoenix. The new position, Deep Throat said, was an innocuous post and had nothing to do with needing Lincoln in the Phoenix area office. It was to get Lincoln out of the Navajo area office and replace him with a yes-man as Navajo area director.

Deep Throat continued, "It was an unfortunate incident. Commissioner Thompson thought he was complying with the wishes of the entire Navajo Nation, not just MacDonald." Unfortunately, it seemed like the commissioner just didn't do his political homework. He trusted what he was told but did not verify it. In other words, he screwed up. MacDonald did not speak for the tribal council. The official governing body of the Navajo Nation spoke for itself. In reality, the chairman did not consult, much less inform, the council when he unilaterally requested that Thompson oust Lincoln.

Anyway, Deep Throat said the real reason why Sneaky Pete (as Roy Bekis from Mitton Rock characterized the slippery chairman) wanted the area director out was because he protested MacDonald's tendency to sign mineral lease agreements without tribal council approval. Furthermore, "there were reports, too, that MacDonald has given the AFL-CIO free reign on the reservation, ordering closed shops without council authority." So, Thompson's transfer order, as beautifully played by MacDonald, was a means to an end.

The only interests served by Lincoln's removal were Big Mac, Big Industry, and Big Labor.

It was a scandal, and Fred and Don had the documents to prove it!

On the night of January 6, Fred Johnson, Don Noble, Lincoln-appointed BIA liaison officer Clare Thompson, and veteran pilot Jimmy Vaughn were killed in a mysterious small airplane crash near Grants. The documents Fred and Don were carrying were allegedly not found by authorities at the plane crash site.

There were also conflicting reports of the plane's flight plan from Albuquerque. One report stated that the plane was scheduled to fly from Albuquerque to Gallup. Another reported that the plane was scheduled to fly from Albuquerque to Window Rock. There were also conflicting reports about the cause of the plane crash. One said adverse weather conditions, another said pilot error, and a third claimed mechanical failure.

Suspecting foul play, we worked with Jim Toulouse, who hired two private airplane crash investigators to examine the wreckage. Although there was no physical evidence of sabotage, one of the investigators said that it was possible for a knowledgeable and experienced saboteur to quietly slip into the Coronado Airfield and neatly cut the plane's fuel line before it took off so that the plane would gradually run out of fuel and go down between Albuquerque and Gallup or Window Rock.

Evidently terrorized, Lincoln accepted Thompson's transfer order, and the majority of the obviously spooked tribal council backed down from its once strong position of self-determination and defected in droves to MacDonald's camp.

Five months later, the reporter Don Bolles was assassinated by organized crime figures in a car explosion in Phoenix. At least one of the assassins had dangerous ties to a ring of white extremist spies who had infiltrated the interior of the Navajo reservation and were totally dedicated to and fanatically working toward the destabilization and eventual violent overthrow of the MacDonald-chaired Navajo tribal government. They planned a future takeover and administration of the tribal reservation by the BIA through the declaration and imposition of federal martial law.

Great! Now we had to worry about the mafia and probably the damn KKK too.

Things were getting very skewed.

CHAPTER 7

THE DANGEROUS ENEMY

Of course, I suspected foul play in the deaths of Fred Johnson and the other three brave men from the Navajo reservation who went down in the small twin-engine aircraft southeast of Grants on the night of January 6, 1976. The accident, apparently by design, occurred on the last leg of the return trip from Washington, DC, where Mr. Johnson's delegation had met a day earlier with Thomas Kleppe and Morris Thompson about the ordered transfer of Tony Lincoln and related issues.

Fred once called himself "the most hated man in Farmington." Although hated by the local bordertown trash, he was loved and respected by his people—the beautiful red people of the five-fingered clan—for his strong and fearless leadership against white racism and exploitation in the Energy Capital of the West. He was chosen by the people of Shiprock and Beclabito to represent the heart of the Northern Navajo Nation and he boldly took those leadership qualities to the Navajo capital in Window Rock. He had a tremendous impact on the tribal political process during the next twelve months, but it was also a year of living dangerously. Then, he was gone. Eliminated, I believe, by his enemies. He, like Larry Casuse, was irreplaceable.

The day after Fred's death, a spokesman for the now-leaderless Navajo tribal council reflected on the significance of the loss and commented that Mr. Johnson was "the most outspoken leader of the

Navajo Nation." In my opinion, he had great potential to become the next tribal chairman. I hoped that he would run for chairman in 1978, but all that changed in an instant.

In our work, we live with danger every day. We are up against mighty giants. If they think we pose too much of a threat, they will move against us. Fred knew that. He also knew that it was better to die on your feet than to live on your knees. He told me about the death threats he received in the energy boomtown of Farmington during the long hot summer of '74. Anonymous messages warned, "If you don't stop leading those marches that are hurting our business, you're going to be the fourth body found." Under his courageous leadership, we kept marching, and downtown businesses in the Western energy capital continued to suffer. Fred later gave me an arrowhead necklace and a leather bag of corn pollen for protection against the relentless gangs of industrial cartels, organized labor syndicates, and shadow government thugs.

In the early spring of 1974, I told Gerald Wilkinson that I was working with Fred on the controversial Exxon uranium lease. Gerry told me to be careful because he had heard that former Papago tribal attorney Edward Berger was working with Peter MacDonald and George Vlassis to get a corporate lease excluded from the National Environmental Policy Act's environmental impact statement requirements. Gerry said that Berger had received a NEPA exclusion for a controversial copper lease on the Papago reservation in Arizona. The Papago citizens strongly opposed the NEPA exclusion on behalf of the copper company and successfully pressured their tribal council to force the non-Indian lawyer to resign. However, in the course of their dark and bloody campaign for reservation environmental protection, the tribal citizens lost three of their four lead organizers. They were assassinated. The citizens also suspected that their tribal chairman, Thomas Segundo, who died in a mysterious small airplane crash in 1971, was also assassinated by pro-copper development forces.

Late one night in the summer of 1974, Fred and I caught a Hispanic male subject trying to put something in my family's mailbox in Farmington. After we confronted him, he identified himself as Nick Saiz. He said that he was a state police investigator and was only trying to read the address on the box. He then offered to set up a meeting between Governor Bruce King and CNL. We then told him that we were already meeting with Governor King and his chief of staff Frank DiLuzio. We also told him that we would report the mailbox incident to our attorney Jim Toulouse, the federal Civil Rights Commission, and the Justice Department. We later told our attorney that Saiz might have been trying to put a pipe bomb in the box.

I also told Pedro Archuleta of the Tierra Amarilla Land Grant about our late-night encounter with Nick Saiz. Pedro said that Saiz was an enemy of the people and the land and to watch out for him. During the 1967 Tierra Amarilla Courthouse Raid, Archuleta and the other Chicano land grant liberators had to shoot and wound then-state police officer Nick Saiz because he presented a clear and present danger to their legitimate citizen's arrest action. When I told Junella Haynes about the mailbox incident, she said that Nick Saiz was observed hanging around the UNM Native American Studies Center in late February and early March of 1973. She also told me to be careful and to never underestimate the agents of repression.

Another state police agent, Tim Chapa, admitted to spying on IAE in Gallup in 1973 and CNL in Farmington in 1974. He also admitted—during a taped interview with myself, David Correia (UNM professor and expert on police repression of Chicano and Indian rights organizations), and Lauro Silva (Chicano civil rights attorney), that he had helped set up the assassination of two Chicano Black Beret activists by state police in Albuquerque's South Valley in 1972. Chapa also admitted he spied on Alianza Federal de Mercedes and El Grito Del Norte in the late sixties and early seventies. I was probably also spied on when I met with Chicano cooperative developer Maria Varela of Tierra Amarilla in 1973 (for technical assistance on the Diné Bi Tsi Yishtilizhii Bii Cooperative in Gallup) and Pedro Archuleta in 1974 (to get intel on Nick Saiz). I also developed a working relationship with El Grito Del Norte and the Chicano

Communications Center to advance crucial solidarity linkages with our natural allies at a time of great common oppression and I was probably spied on during that time as well.

I also had several direct encounters with the Farmington city police (the last time I was in their custody, they threatened to kill me) and members of the San Juan County Sheriff's Office (whose jurisdiction was supposed to be rural San Juan County, not urban Farmington) in the early summer of 1974. The encounters occurred as I walked to and from my internship at EOC. After I reported the encounters to Jim Toulouse and John Dulles II of the Civil Rights Commission, the encounters stopped. There were also some open death threats made, but Gerry told me how to deal with those.

Later, we caught an admitted FBI informant trying to infiltrate our NIYC CETA program and promptly dropped him from the program client list. We then caught another informant (also operating under the cover of a CETA program client) snooping around the office at night. We got rid of him too. There were also a couple of overnight office break-ins but no suspects. These guys were getting better. All this strange shit was not happening in isolation. By late 1975, it was clear that we, as an organization, were being directly targeted by sinister elements. As primary direct human targets, Gerry and I weren't really surprised, though. We were expecting it.

———

Uncompromising Indian rights work is not for the faint of heart.

I knew Don Noble but didn't know him as well as Fred Johnson. A nephew of Annie Wauneka, Don served as president of the twenty-six-chapter Fort Defiance Agency Council, was a two-term chairman of the Navajo Tribal Council Judiciary Committee, and the chairman of the tribal council committee established to review the legality of the AFL-CIO agreements. Even before I met Don, I respected and admired him. I remember on March 1, 1973, when Don publicly issued a strong and courageous statement supporting the reasons behind what Navajo human rights warriors Larry Casuse and Robert Nakaidinae did what they had to do on the streets of Gallup earlier that day. Don spoke for the People then, and he would continue to work and fight for their tribal rights for the rest of his life.

I didn't personally know Clare Thompson, but I knew that he was a longtime Navajo tribal council interpreter. He had also worked with the Navajo-Hopi Land Dispute Commission and the Office of Navajo Political Affairs. In 1974, he helped direct the Navajo Tribe-AFL-CIO COPE voter registration and turnout drive against Barry Goldwater and other politicians supporting Navajo relocation. The following year, Tony Lincoln appointed Mr. Thompson as BIA tribal operations specialist for the Navajo area office (NAO). As the NAO tribal operations specialist, he served as a liaison between the BIA and the Navajo Tribe. It was in this capacity as a liaison that he attended the January 5 meeting in DC. Like his superior, Tony Lincoln, Clare Thompson had insisted on tribal fiscal restraint and open government. They pushed for balanced tribal budgets and government in the sunshine.

A longtime Window Rock resident, Jimmy Vaughn owned and operated the reservation-based Orlando Flying Service that served the Navajo Tribe and provided direct tribal flight service to and from Albuquerque and other area destinations. His daughter Carol Vaughn-Lankford later called and told me that her father was a former Air Force major and an experienced military and civilian pilot with an excellent flight record. It seemed to me that the government's theory of pilot error as a cause for the airplane crash was in itself in error. In fact, it looked like part of a larger cover-up.

Fred and I had planned to meet in Farmington on January 7. We were also scheduled to testify at a public hearing at city hall in Farmington on New Mexico's Senator Pete Domenici's plan to resurrect congressional coal gasification loan guarantee legislation that Congress had failed to pass in December. We, of course, were going to testify against planned legislation to provide $6 billion in federal loan guarantees to the coal gas industry. WESCO and CONPASO were already ready to restate their obscene corporate welfare position that commercial coal gasification would not be economically viable unless they received government loan guarantees. The original legislation passed in the Senate but did not pass in the House of Representatives in late 1975 due in part to the coordinated opposition from NIYC, CNL, AIM, and the Shiprock Research Center.

The legislation was largely crafted by new Texas Eastern Transmission Corporation governmental affairs manager Jerry Verkler, a longtime staff director of the Senate Interior and Insular Affairs Committee. Sponsoring the legislation in the Senate was Senator Henry "Scoop" Jackson, the longtime chairman of the Interior and Insular Affairs committee. Shortly after the Senate bill was introduced, it was amended to provide 80 percent of the taxpayer-backed federal loan guarantees to Texas Eastern Transmission Corporation. Although the bill's amendment was controversial, Senator Scoop Jackson refused to hold a hearing on it. His former committee staff director Jerry Verkler (aka Little Scoop) and his new corporate employer, the designated primary beneficiary of the amended bill, probably didn't want a hearing on it either. The controversial amendment was co-sponsored by Senator Domenici.

Jerry Verkler was chief of staff of the Senate Interior and Insular Affairs Committee from 1963 to 1975 and by December of '75 became a lobbyist for Texas Eastern Transmission Corporation. In 1963, the Department of Interior Office of Coal Research contracted with Consolidation Coal Company to construct and operate a pilot coal gasification plant in the Appalachia Mountains. According to their $9 million contract, the pilot plant was designed to advance the coal gasification technology process so that it could be applied on a commercial scale in nominated coal reserve territories like Burnham, where "the El Paso (Natural) Gas Company holds a lease which is not yet in operation as research is underway on the manufacture of by-products from coal. There are different technical problems to solve in this research, but the potential when the problems are solved are considered very great. The El Paso Company also plans to use the coal for gas purposes."

In 1968, Consolidation Coal Company joined El Paso Natural Gas Company as joint leaseholders of forty thousand coal acres of land in Burnham. The Interior Department (which housed the Office of Coal Research and the pro-coal development Bureau of Mines) gave final federal approval on the lease for the two coal companies. Three years later, El Paso announced plans to construct and operate three of the nation's first, and world's largest, commercial coal gasification plants on the Burnham lease. However, the lease was due to expire in 1978 on its own terms. Earlier in November 1975, El Paso and Consol tried to get the Navajo tribal council to extend the term of the lease so that it could be mined to provide coal for the three coal gasification plants that would have an operating life of twenty-five years.

However, under Fred's strong leadership, the tribal council voted to table the lease extension proposal because there were too many unanswered questions and unresolved issues associated with the proposed mining and gasification project. Peter Mac blindly supported the unsound project (even offering to give the El Paso gassers thirty thousand acre-feet of tribal water per year) and wanted the council to reconsider the tabled proposal in January 1976. However, it didn't make any sense to bring the proposal back up because coal gasification was not economically viable without a multi-billion dollar federal loan guarantee program which Congress, in its wisdom, decided not to legislate a month earlier. So, the gasification-based lease extension proposal was premature. A request for tribal action on the proposal was more than premature. It was imprudent—in every way.

I was going to testify on all that and more. But when I heard the airplane carrying Fred Johnson, Don Noble, Clare Thompson, and Jimmy Vaughn was missing, I immediately canceled my plans to go to Farmington. Instead, I met with Jim Toulouse and together, we contacted Fred's wife, Mary in Shiprock.

To be clear, Fred, Don, and I were not totally anti-union. We were opposed to the presence of the AFL-CIO on the reservation because its duplicitous deals with Chairman MacDonald were directly related to planned coal gasification and uranium development which we opposed. That didn't mean that we were completely insensitive to the concerns of the Navajo working man and working woman. In 1974, one of CNL's strongholds existed among the Navajo women who worked at the Fairchild plant in Shiprock. I will always remember that summer day when Fred, Wilbert Tsosie, and I went to meet with management to address critical worker issues at the plant. All the one thousand women employees on the electronics assembly lines stopped and gave us a long, enthusiastic standing ovation. They saw us as champions of their worker rights.

With Fred's help, Don launched a campaign to independently and locally unionize the Shiprock Fairchild plant workers. While the initial effort fell short of its ambitious goal, it represented a good start in terms of uniting the workers to at least participate in the process of collective bargaining. Although Fred and Don supported the tribal right to work law, they kept an open mind on Navajo labor organizing from the inside. They didn't have a problem with the need for "proper" internal human resource development and utilization on the rez ("proper" meaning no more coal and uranium "slavery wages"). Existing plants like Fairchild and General Dynamics were alright, especially the pro-CNL Shiprock facility. A week before his death, Fred said, "If the people want a union, then fine. Who knows? Maybe we could start our own, the way the United Farm Workers did."

———

After we buried Fred in Shiprock and Don in Ganado, it was time to reassess things and make some adjustments. We no longer had a majority in the tribal council—a hard reality that defined or limited our political work on the coal gasification and AFL-CIO issues. Realistically, we would have to do most of our work from the outside. The Tony Lincoln issue was now a non-issue after his acceptance of the transfer order. The related self-determination argument was also reduced to a non-issue with Tony's acceptance of the new BIA regional position, which in an apparent compromise with his great white father superiors, was created in the Albuquerque area office, not the Phoenix area office. There would be no political or legal challenges to the transfer order. A challenge wouldn't have been very effective anyway.

The absolutely indispensable leadership team of Fred and Don was now gone and the original documents Fred had were missing. I didn't know if there was a meeting or meetings with Barry Goldwater and other members of Congress in DC on the morning of January 6. Fred, Don, and Annie Wauneka had written letters on the Tony Lincoln and AFL-CIO issues. I also didn't know if Fred gave Don Bolles copies of the documents. If he did, was Don going to do something with them as an investigative reporter? Maybe Fred gave him copies, but before he could do something with them, he got whacked by the mafia in Phoenix in early June.

One thing I did know, however, was that we now had to reallocate our organizational resources to fight coal and uranium on Navajo. I closed the NIYC lobbying office in Window Rock and hired Esther Keeswood to open and direct our new field office in Shiprock. We would still fight coal gasification but turn it into more of a protracted ground war. We would grind the bastards—coal gas bastards—down.

I didn't think we had the angle to properly address the AFL-CIO issue as an outside NGO. We had only supported Don and Fred. Now what? I respected Annie Wauneka but I didn't want to work with Barry Goldwater. He may have opposed the AFL-CIO but probably supported coal gasification and Exxon. He philosophically preferred the use of "company unions" over worker unions (such as the AFL-CIO and their legitimate anti-Goldwater Committee on Political Education). I didn't want to work with company unions. This stuff was getting too hairy, so I decided we should just stay out of the internal union issue. Our true position was that we opposed everybody—Big Industry, Big Labor, puppet tribal governments, Barry Goldwater, and company unions. Keep it simple, I always say.

The Exxon issue was different. It was more legal than political. Our strategy was to force the Bureau of Indian Affairs to do an EIS, however inadequate. Then, we would sue them for their inadequate EIS. It was a delay tactic—but a delay tactic which could kill if done right. At least that's what the white environmental crazies (Gerry's term for them) claimed. A resourceful NGO with standing could skillfully manipulate NEPA to kill off a fair number of deserving projects or undertakings by deploying an extended series of legal smart bombs intended to keep the sad sack EIS preparers in court for the next hundred years. That's longer than a ninety-nine-year lease! It's certainly longer than a prudent company on a realistic project deadline would wait for a final environmental impact statement and a legally unchallengeable record of decision.

There was an art and science to being a successful obstructionist according to the anti-development theory. But then we're talking Exxon here. Any thoughtful power analysis would suggest that the real enemy is the number one corporation on the Fortune 500 (in 1976), not the incompetent BIA or the lowest bidder who writes the EIS reports. Yes, it would be Exxon, the project developer and likely defendant-intervenor in whatever EIS court case is filed. Herb Blatchford, the oldest and wisest, gave us a serious reality check. He stated unequivocally that Exxon owned all the judges in America, including the Supremes. An ultimately successful EIS challenge directly involving Exxon's corporate interests would be most challenging. It was true, and we needed to hear it.

———

In February, I had just returned from speaking to the Appalachia Coalition (a regional anti-coal strip-mining alliance) at the Highlander Research and Education Center in New Market, Tennessee. Gerry sent me a cryptic message that he was waiting for me at the Albuquerque International Airport main bar. I had already called JoAllan and told her not to wait up. After the skycap delivered my luggage, Gerry and I went to Enrico's for dinner and then to the Bird of Paradise for a few drinks after dinner. It was somewhere between the eighth and ninth pitcher that he told me that Jack Crowder was a spy for Barry Goldwater, who plotted to overthrow Peter MacDonald as Navajo tribal council chairman in late 1975 and early 1976 so that then-BIA Navajo area director Tony

Lincoln could take over the administration of the Navajo tribe and reservation. Gerry said he was shocked when he got the information from his source, code-named DD. He never told me the real names of his sources and I didn't ask. I had sources too, but I just called them all Deep Throat or DT. I wasn't a complicated man.

I first met Jack Crowder or JC when I was hitchhiking from Gallup to Window Rock in the summer of 1973. He picked me up across from Little Bear's and we chatted a bit. He said he was from Bernalillo and had co-authored a Navajo children's book entitled *Stephannie and the Coyote*. From the way he talked, it seemed like he already knew who I was. Maybe that's why he picked me up, I thought, as we hot-rodded past the "South Erection Site" of the expanding McKinley Mine. After he dropped me off at the Council House, I thanked him for the ride and shook his hand.

I didn't think about Jack until the spring of 1975 when Junella Haynes mentioned that she had recently met him at an Indian education conference in Albuquerque and he said he knew me. In the fall of 1975, Tom Luebben brought Jack to the office to meet Gerry and me. Tom said that Jack was going to help us on our new Intermountain Boarding School case. The first thing Jack said when he saw me was, "Remember me?" I said, "Yeah, I remember. You gave me a ride to Window Rock a couple years ago. And you showed me that book you wrote" (actually co-wrote—my bad). We shook hands again.

As we talked some more, it turned out that Jack was a consultant for the Navajo Area School Board Association (NASBA) in Window Rock. He knew a lot about the BIA and how it worked—how it really worked. Later, Tom Heidlebaugh, who used to work for Rough Rock Demonstration School, told me some rather strange things about NASBA. Although he didn't know Jack, he knew of him. The way he said it and his tense body language indicated that there might be another side, a dark side, to Jack. I wanted to talk to Tom more about Jack Crowder and NASBA but regrettably, it never happened.

In the late fall of 1975, I was invited to attend an anti-AFL CIO caucus meeting in Jack Crowder's office at NASBA. So, I jumped on the back of a Greyhound and got there in no time. The meeting was about AFL-CIO agreements. Jack knew the agreements inside and out and called them self-serving sweetheart deals between Big Industry and Big Labor. In particular, he noted how the $25 million HRDI (Human Resource Development Institute) contract represented a gross misuse of tribal and federal manpower funds. He gave a truly substantive presentation and I really liked his analysis. Maybe he really was just trying to help, like the time he gave me a ride to Window Rock or when he came to our Albuquerque office on a weekend to assist us in the meticulous preparation of our Intermountain case. He seemed to have the best of intentions. I remember thinking that Tom had to be wrong about this fine gent. Boy, was I a real babe in the woods! Now I know that it's the well-intentioned, eager-beaver ones that you have to watch out for. After hearing DD's revelations, I suspected I was more naive than I thought.

———

Gerry told me that DD began at the beginning, and the beginning began with Barry Goldwater, who ran Goldwater's Department Store in Phoenix that he inherited from his father, Baron, who inherited it from his wealthy father (Barry's grandfather), Michael, who established the capitalist enterprise when Arizona was still a territory. Barry reportedly didn't run the family business very well, so his close friend, Harry Rosenzweig of Rosenzweig Jewelers in Phoenix, helped get him into politics. Soon, Barry and Harry were on the still corrupt Phoenix City Council. After Barry went into politics, his brother Robert took over Goldwater's Department Store. He ran the store so successfully that Goldwater's soon became a major stockholder of the Valley National Bank in Phoenix, which was headed by Walter Bimson, a friend of Robert and Barry. Then Robert was appointed to the bank's board of directors.

Barry, Harry, and Robert were all business partners and did a lot of business with well-known organized crime figures in Arizona,

Nevada, and California. They also befriended and partnered with real estate developer Del Webb (of Del Webb Construction Company in Phoenix), who also did a lot of business with shady characters in seamy Phoenix and Las Vegas. Del was another board member of Valley National Bank, which financed his vast empire in the Southwest. Del's regional building empire included the Flamingo Casino in Las Vegas for mobster Bugsy Siegel, the development of Sun City (a master-planned retirement community) in the Valley of the Sun for a bunch of rich white bluehairs from back East, and the construction of the Poston War Relocation Center (a World War II civilian concentration camp) for the unconstitutional internment of Japanese-American citizens who were forcibly removed from their homes and businesses on the West Coast for settlement on the already-intertribally settled Colorado River Indian reservation near Parker.

Banker Bimson also befriended Frank Snell (of the Snell and Wilmer law firm of Phoenix), who represented Valley National Bank and was also on the board. He was involved in creating Arizona Public Service Company of Phoenix—then the state's largest utility company—and served as its board chairman.

Barry co-owned the Rainbow Lodge and Trading Post at the base of the sacred Navajo Mountain. It accommodated endless mule trains of ignorant and disrespectful tourists on their way to desecrate the sacred Rainbow Bridge with their inappropriate presence. He acquired the co-ownership as a gift from his wife Margaret to celebrate their wedding anniversary. To show appreciation and increase the volume of sacrilegious overland tourist traffic on the widened Rainbow Trail, he contracted with his friend and business partner, Del Webb, to improve the property by constructing a long runway at the Rainbow Airport. In 1951, the improved property burned down. Local folklore held that Barry always blamed local Navajos. One of Barry's hobbies was collecting sacred Hopi Kachina Dolls—hundreds of them—a macabre hobby he had since he was seven years old. Bad Navajos, good Hopis who generously shared with little Bahana. That probably explains why he always took the Hopi position in the Navajo-Hopi Land Dispute.

———

Suddenly, it was two o'clock in the morning so Gerry and I changed our venue from the Bird of Paradise to Kap's, an all-night coffee shop on East Central. Over a couple of short stacks and a hot pot of Juan Valdez's best, we continued.

The so-called Navajo-Hopi land dispute involved reservation lands created by the 1882 executive order and the 1934 executive order. The lands were home to both Navajo and Hopi tribal members. There were more Navajos than Hopis, so the Navajos occupied and used most of the joint executive order reservation lands. Surrounding the Hopis, in a good way, the powerful Navajos provided a buffer to protect their smaller pueblo neighbors from harmful outside non-Indian encroachment. Without that friendly protective buffer, the vulnerable Hopis would have been swiftly overrun by Mormons and other encroaching non-Indians. Fortunately, though, the Navajos were a large land-based tribe and growing.

Located within the so-called land dispute area was Black Mesa Basin, which held "maximum opportunities for the development of . . . reserves of uranium, coal, petroleum, natural gas, and helium." The problem with maximizing development opportunities was that non-Indian interests wanted to lease and exploit the Indian executive order reservation lands but couldn't because they didn't know which tribe owned and could, therefore, lease the subject lands. So, it was the frustrated corporate interests that created the legal fiction of an intertribal land dispute.

As Gerry and I continued, we were joined by a third party who came in from the cold. DD wore a warm trench coat with faded initial lettering on the right collar, and sat with his back to the wall. At first, he listened. Then, he spoke; actually, it was more of a whisper, like he had gauze in his mouth.

In 1952, three major events occurred that established the legislative and judicial course of the alleged Navajo-Hopi land dispute. First, the Arizona Public Service Company was created and began looking for coal to fuel the power plants it wanted to build. The company looked at the Black Mesa Coal Field, which held an estimated twenty-one billion tons of coal. But the large coal field was inaccessible because of the unresolved land dispute status.

Second, Barry Goldwater became a US senator with a little help from the new Arizona State Republican Party chairman, Henry Rosenzweig. Arizona political allies Richard Kleindienst and Robert Mardian (of the infamous Watergate Scandal) also helped secure the pivotal Winslow bloc vote. Non-Arizona political allies, H.L. Hunt and another super-rich Texas oilman, were among Goldwater's major investors—I mean major contributors. Although Barry was supposed to be anti-union, he accepted a campaign contribution of $5,000 "from a convicted labor racketeer who would later be murdered gangland style for running afoul of Las Vegas interests." Although the racketeer Willie Bioff "was close to Goldwater" and "had launched Goldwater's political career by giving Rosenzweig" the money "for Goldwater's first senate campaign," he was offed by a car bomb.

"What the hell was DD getting at?" I wondered out loud. Well, Barry Goldwater did, through his family business, have "Las Vegas interests" like "former Cleveland mobster Moe Dalitz," who gave the Goldwaters "the exclusive franchise for their department store in Dalitz's Las Vegas hotel and casino, the Desert Inn." Hmmm. Close or closer? Help me out here, DD—if that's your real name. Whisper louder! I offered a good hint. Wasn't it the Godfather who said, "Keep your friends and interests close, but your enemies closer"? And I'm getting closer—oh shit, I shouldn't have said that . . . Goldwater considered labor unions corrupt and, therefore, the enemy. Like that racketeer.

Third, the major case of *Arizona v. California* began. Representing the State of Arizona in the historic Colorado River water rights adjudication case was Frank Snell of Snell and Wilmer, one of the Big Three in Phoenix's political and business power elite. The landmark case would later be called "the greatest water rights litigation of the West."

In 1956, Senator Barry Goldwater and Representative Stewart Udall sponsored bills in Congress to authorize the federal government to solve part of the Navajo-Hopi Land Dispute so that private industry (such as Arizona Public Service Company) could lease and develop the Indian mineral estate in the Black Mesa Basin in the 1882 executive order reservation. The bills were at the behest of former Utah US Attorney and current Hopi tribal lawyer John Boyden. He maliciously prosecuted Navajos for resisting the BIA-supervised livestock reduction in the BIA-designated grazing districts two, eight, and nine that stretched from Navajo Mountain to Aneth during the Navajo Holocaust from 1933 to 1945. The Goldwater-Udall legislation was based on the severance of Traditional Life and Land in the Fourth World. To remove the minerals from the leased lands, required forcing the people and their livestock from their homes and grazing areas.

The congressional legislation did not pass in 1956 and the BIA lamented, "For some twenty-five years, oil companies have been interested in exploring the oil and gas potential of the Black Mesa Basin, a region lying within the area of the executive order of 1882, the ownership of which is in dispute between the Navajo and Hopi Tribes. It is a very promising area, and one that is expected to produce a high income when, with its ownership finally determined, development leasing becomes possible by the Tribe concerned." (The "high income" for the non-Indian companies and low royalties for the Indian tribes.)

In 1957, Arizona's Barry Goldwater and Stewart Udall reintroduced their legislation. The Department of the Interior proposed an amendment that would provide an interim leasing provision. Congressman Udall supported the proposed amendment "that undoubtedly will be included in the bill" when it "is finally enacted." In a letter to Representative Udall, that was copied by Walter

Bimson of Phoenix's Big Three, Thomas Shiya of Valley National Bank wrote, "A number of us have wondered for some time why it would be not possible for applying a formula that would enable the Bureau of Indian Affairs to lease the Hopi-Navajo disputed lands while the oil boom (occurring on undisputed Navajo lands northeast of the 1882 executive order reservation) is accelerating with monies put in a special fund [at Valley National Bank, no doubt] until the dispute is settled. I see that your bill is providing exactly that kind of answer." The "formula" Shiya suggested could easily be amended to include coal, uranium, natural gas, and helium in addition to oil.

On the matter of Indian overlay disposal, the coal industry's brute extractive approach—its open pit, its strip mining, its mountain top removal, and its making of a national sacrifice area—wanted all Navajo and Hopi residents on coal reserve lands removed and relocated. The industry also had a lot of infrastructure (associated processing and transportation systems such as coal preparation plants, conveyor belts, slurry pipelines, railroad spurs, haulage roads, etc.) to get into place on prospective lease and rights-of-way areas. Arizona Public Service Company (APS) "engaged" Stanford Research Institute to develop a series of development scenarios to begin as early as 1958. APS and Stanford simply assumed the depopulation of planned coal resource areas and mining pits would have already taken place.

In 1958, Senator Goldwater and Representative *and* Mormon attorney (yes, that's relevant) Stewart Udall got their legislative bill passed to settle the Navajo-Hopi Land Dispute. This version of the legislation authorized the Hopis to sue the Navajos in a special federal district court to determine the ownership and control of the surface and subsurface estates on the 1882 executive order reservation, and the lease-ability of its mineral estate. The Hopi Tribe then sued the Navajo Tribe. The Hopis were represented by their non-Indian tribal lawyer and Mormon Bishop John Boyden. Per authorizing legislation, Boyden then "joined a reputable Arizona firm on the complaint." The law firm was Fennemore, Craig, Allen, and McClennen—of which Stewart Udall's Mormon cousin Calvin was a member. The Navajos were represented by white tribal attorney Norman Littell, who had also represented the tribe in lease negotiations with Arizona Public Service Company.

APS, partly owned by the Mormon Church, wanted to build their Four Corners Power Plant near Nenahnezad and Spencer Chemical Company (later Pittsburgh-Midway Coal Mining Company) to mine coal at the McKinley Mine near Black Hat to fuel APS's Cholla Power Plant near Joseph City, named after Mormon Church founder Joseph Smith. Congressman Stewart Udall later introduced congressional legislation that authorized a ninety-nine-year lease for APS to operate the Four Corners Power Plant fueled by coal mined by Utah Construction Company (later Utah Construction and Mining Company), which was unsurprisingly founded, financed, and directed by Utah Mormons. The Hopi Tribe's lawsuit trial was held in Prescott—a Mormon outlier—in 1960.

Even though the case was not yet decided, Fisher Contracting Company of Phoenix somehow got a lease from the Hopi Tribe for thirty-six thousand acres of land in Hopi district six within the 1882 executive order reservation for coal exploration, possible mining, and a possible mine-mouth power plant. District six was a BIA-designated grazing district—a designation that applied to the surface, not the subsurface or mineral estate. The imbecilic BIA approved the coal lease anyway, as did Stewart Udall, who was now the Secretary of Interior.

Del Fisher, the board president of Fisher Contracting Company, was also a board director of Arizona Public Service Company, whose board chairman Frank Snell was also a board director of Fisher Contracting Company. A pretty fishy arrangement there.

In 1962, the special federal district court three-judge panel decided that Hopi district six was now exclusive Hopi reservation land and, therefore, leasable by the Hopi Tribe. One of the special district court judges was James Walsh, a former member of the Snell and Wilmer law firm that had connections with APS and Fisher.

The non-Indian court also decided that the rest of the 1882 Indian executive order reservation was a joint Navajo and Hopi reservation. If the Navajo and Hopi tribes wanted to co-lease their joint land resources, then they could. So, the pressure was on the tribes to lease their joint mineral estate. Representing the tribes were white tribal lawyers who had their own unethical agendas fraught with naked conflicts of interest.

———

Soon it was six o'clock in the morning and our discussion was still in the early sixties. "Hey, DD. We gotta leave. Gerry and I have a national organization to run, you know."

In 1963, the US Supreme Court affirmed the special federal district court decision on the lease-ability of Hopi district six and the Navajo Hopi joint use area.

That same day, the Supreme Court ruled in another matter strategically linked to the lease-ability in the joint use area and Joseph City, where Arizona Public Service Company had constructed and operated the Cholla Power Plant. The plant was cooled by a large industrial reservoir fed by the Little Colorado River (a major tributary of the Colorado River)—the subject of the landmark *Arizona v. California* water rights case. Frank Snell successfully represented the State of Arizona in this historic Supreme Court case. It was Snell who helped make the decision to build the large power plant and cooling reservoir at Joseph City in his capacity as APS board member.

Fisher Contracting Company formally expressed interest in leasing and the development of coal in the Navajo-occupied Cow Springs area of the non-district-six portion of the 1882 executive order reservation, possibly with an eye towards mining the coal in the Cow Springs area to help supply APS's Cholla Power Plant when it expanded. Pretty soon, a suggestion was made on Capitol Hill to "partition" the coal-rich joint use area and "kick the Navajos off."

In late 1963, the first partition and relocation legislation was introduced but did not pass because Barry Goldwater was too busy campaigning for president. In 1964, the Salt River Project of

Phoenix was trying to get water from Arizona's share of the Upper Colorado River to build a power plant at LeChee near Page (near the proposed Cow Springs coal lease area) as part of Secretary Stewart Udall's WEST Associates' Grand Plan. In a major case to determine the ownership of the Salt River Project (which would later operate the LeChee plant as a part-owner), it was represented by Jennings, Strouss, Salmon, and Trask—of which Stewart's Mormon cousin Nicholas was a member. One of the Arizona Supreme Court judges deciding the significant case was Nicholas' Mormon uncle Jesse. The Udall Clan had lawyers all over the place, including at Tucson Gas and Electric Company, another eventual part-owner of the power plant at LeChee (and partly owned by APS and other private and public utilities).

Salt River was having trouble getting the water because the Navajo Tribe had "prior and paramount" Winters Doctrine rights to the Arizona portion of the Upper Colorado River. To get Navajo water, Secretary Udall refused to approve the contract to deliver water from the Navajo Dam to the congressionally authorized Navajo Indian Irrigation Project in New Mexico until the Navajo Tribe waived its water rights so that Salt River could build its power plant at LeChee. Udall justified his blackmail tactic by pointing to language in the 1963 US Supreme Court decision in *Arizona v. California* that stated, "we have held that the Secretary is vested with considerable control over the apportionment of Colorado River waters."

In 1964, Peabody Coal Company proposed a power plant at Antelope Creek near Page. The company also proposed a power plant at Paiute Farms. Representing Peabody, John Boyden "urged" the Utah State Land Board at a hearing to "sell" land to the company so that it could build its Paiute Farms Power Plant. The land was probably Navajo-occupied and used state land located within the checkerboarded Utah portion of the Navajo reservation. That same year, Boyden represented Peabody at a hearing of the Utah State Water and Power Board. He "argued" in support of the company's intent to "obtain" water rights from the State of Utah. Again,

Peabody wanted Utah state water rights for its proposed Paiute Farms Power Plant, but the Navajo Tribe had "prior and paramount" Winters Doctrine rights to the Utah portion of the San Juan River that was a major tributary of the Upper Colorado River. I guess John Boyden and Mr. Peabody wanted the State of Utah to challenge the tribe's reserved rights to the Utah part of the San Juan River.

Boyden was also a member of the Utah State Commission on Indian Affairs, which was successfully sued by Utah Navajos for gross mismanagement of state trust funds intended for their use and benefit in the Aneth Extension. Now, he wanted the state to take away Utah Navajo water and give it to Peabody. The proposed Antelope Creek and Paiute Farms power plant project was also located near the proposed Cow Springs coal lease area and Peabody's twenty-five-thousand-acre coal mining lease on exclusive Navajo reservation land at Black Mesa.

In 1962, Secretary Stewart Udall approved a seventy-five-thousand-acre coal exploration lease for Peabody. After the company explored for coal on the leasehold, it proposed to mine coal on twenty-five thousand acres within the exploration lease area. Secretary Udall approved Peabody's proposed twenty-five-thousand-acre coal mining lease in 1964. Later, Peabody's proposed Antelope Creek and Paiute Farms power plant project was withdrawn in favor of Salt River's proposed LeChee Power Plant (which, when approved by Secretary Udall, would be fueled by coal mined at Peabody's twenty-five-thousand-acre lease at Black Mesa) and Southern California Edison Company's proposed mine-mouth Kaiparowits Power Plant in Utah (which would be built right across the San Juan River from the withdrawn Paiute Farms Power Plant). Arizona Public Service Company offered to be a part-owner of the proposed Kaiparowits Power Plant until it was abandoned. Southern California Edison Company later proposed a power plant near Bullhead City in Arizona.

Later, Peabody got a fifty-eight-thousand-acre coal drilling lease (which, of course, was approved by Stewart Udall) in the joint use area (JUA) of Black Mesa. After the company drilled for coal on the leasehold, it got a forty-thousand-acre coal mining lease within the drilling lease area (again approved by Stew Udall) for Southern California Edison Company's planned Mohave Power Plant near Bullhead City.

By 1966, Peabody had sixty-five thousand coal acres—forty thousand of which were in the JUA. Then, in 1969–70, the company got a coal exploration and drilling lease for another ten thousand acres in the JUA. By 1970, it had sixty-five thousand coal mining acres and ten thousand coal exploration and drilling acres in the JUA and non-JUA areas on Black Mesa. It looked like Peabody already had a monopoly out there. As the nation's largest coal mining company, it had coal supply agreements to mine four hundred million tons of coal on sixty-five thousand acres. There were also seventy-eight Navajo families or approximately four hundred tribal individuals living on those sixty-five thousand coal acres. And the four hundred million tons of coal on sixty-five thousand acres was only part of a larger coal development plan. A grander Grand Plan existed.

With Stewart Udall now working for the Fennemore law firm, the Arizona Bureau of Mines reported that "Black Mesa . . . contains the most extensive coal reserves in Arizona" and that "the estimated total reserves of coal in the Black Mesa field is near 21 billion . . . tons." The Bureau also reported that "the Four Corners region, including Arizona, appears destined to become part of one of the world's largest energy producing centers." This global forecast drove the push for partition and relocation of the people. In 1970, there were an estimated fifteen thousand Navajos living in the JUA portion of Black Mesa, so part of the final solution was to "partition" the JUA. Kick off 7,500 Navajos and a few Hopis. The ones who are "caught on the wrong side of the line." You have a separate but equal arrangement. Remove over 7,500 Navajos and Hopis off coal surface minable land and that takes care of half of the human overburden problem of the strip minable JUA. Replace the Indian relocatees and their livestock with draglines. DD was being frank, and he knew how the enemy thought and he continued. At that point, equal and undivided rights and interests in the mineral estate were hardly relevant. Assuming undisputed mineral leasing and development, the two tribes can just split the rentals, bonuses, and royalties in half so they can pay their overpaid non-Indian attorneys to represent them in future land disputes created over the ownership and control of the mineral-rich 1934 executive order reservation.

In 1971, John Boyden and Barry Goldwater got together with Arizona congressman Sam Steiger, originally from New York, to get another partition and relocation bill introduced in Congress. Thanks largely to Peter MacDonald's lobbying efforts, the Arizona apartheid legislation did not pass Congress in 1972 and 1973. However, in 1974, Arizona senators Goldwater and Paul Fannin co-sponsored their version of the Steiger bill which Goldwater thought was too generous to the Navajos. Chairman MacDonald got the AFL-CIO involved, but even they couldn't stop Congress from passing it or President Gerald Ford from signing the so-called Navajo-Hopi Land Settlement Act. The 1974 law authorized the Arizona federal district court judge, James Walsh, a former member of the Snell and Wilmer law firm, to partition the surface estate of the Navajo-Hopi JUA and order the relocation of all Navajo and Hopi Indians living on the wrong side of the partition line. The law also established the federal Navajo and Hopi Indian Relocation Commission that was to be directed by Leon Berger "who had once worked for Barry Goldwater."

The coffee kicked in. DD was on a roll. MacDonald didn't seem to have a problem relocating seventy-eight Navajo families off the coal lease area, but he did have a problem with the government relocating 7,500 JUA Navajos living outside of Peabody's leases.

———

DD then moved on to the rumor about Goldwater putting out a contract on MacDonald's life. Even though Goldwater got his congressional revenge against the Navajos for allegedly burning down his exploitive trading post at Navajo Mountain, he was still out to get MacDonald for bringing in the hated AFL-CIO and its equally hated Committee on Political Education (COPE). So, he recruited his close friend Joe Patrick of Phoenix to work with Jack Crowder at NASBA to spy on MacDonald and bring about a regime change using his—and, now, get this—"protégé" Tony Lincoln. Yes, Goldwater's protégé, Tony Lincoln.

Last month, DD's informant told him that Jack, Joe, Barry, and Tony got together in Phoenix in late 1975 (and possibly in Window Rock after that) with some local mafia types by the names of John Adamson, Neal Roberts, and Jimmy Robinson to discuss ways to neutralize or eliminate MacDonald. To terminate the chairman's authority—with extreme prejudice. They came up with different scenarios. Plant a bomb to explode in MacDonald's office or plant a bomb in Tony's car, except fix it so that it doesn't explode, then blame MacDonald for planting the car bomb or ordering the planting of the bomb in Lincoln's Lincoln (actually, MacDonald drove a Lincoln Continental, and Lincoln, well, he better trade his BIA car in for a tank). They also considered blowing up an IHS hospital. Get AIM to take over something. Raise havoc on the rez. Anything to get federal martial law declared and imposed in Window Rock and then install Tony to replace Mac as chairman. All of these scenarios were being discussed while Tony was still the BIA Navajo area director.

Goldwater had previously tried to get Tony to hire Joe at the BIA Navajo area office. When that didn't work out, he got Tony to get Joe hired at NASBA (which is funded by the BIA). That began to explain how Jack was involved in all of this. DD began to wrap it up:

> Personally, I don't think Jack's killer material, but I think that he is being used... You and Gerry pay for the breakfast burritos to go. I'll get the tip. . . . And Jack knows that he's being used but he accepts it. The same thing with Tony. Well, not exactly. Tony's professional and political feud with Mac goes way back to ONEO (Office of Navajo Employment Opportunity) and the Nakai administration years and has manifested itself in myriad ways since. Shit, why can't we all just get along? Oh, and Neal and some of his associates

aren't very happy with what Don Bolles has been writing about them in the 'Arizona Repulsive,' I mean *Republic.* Mafia dog racing stuff. Near as I can tell, it doesn't have anything directly to do with Navajo. That's all I know at this stage. It'll all shake out in about a year. Maybe longer.

But what I do find deeply troubling is that the most outspoken tribal councilman was probably assassinated. And the tribal chairman, the most powerful Indian leader in America, has been put in great danger. That's your two biggest tribal leaders. And Tony—the way he's allowed himself to be used. That's extremely disturbing. One last thing. My informant says that he's not surprised that so many Navajo people are now blaming MacDonald for causing Fred's death. Just the way MacDonald would have been blamed for putting a car bomb in Tony's car. *They*—and you know who I'm talking about—have got the Nation right where they want it. Think about it. With that, I'm outta here.

I had to get going too. I had urgent business in the south. All that time, I didn't know jack about Jack. Or tony about . . . After DD's revelations and analysis, all I knew was that I had to strengthen my working relationship with the REAL PEOPLE. That weekend, I took JoAllan and Kayah to the Manzano Mountains. Ten thousand feet up where the earth touches the sky and the sacred headwaters form. The cold, clear air cleansed my heart and soul and re-centered me for the work ahead.

———

I had been actively involved in the Navajo relocation issue since December 1972 when Mitch Fowler and Penny Hunter asked me to help them assist the one hundred Navajos who were forced to relocate from district six. In the summer of 1974, I worked with the Navajo-Hopi Unity Caravan on its way to Washington, DC to lobby against the partition and relocation legislation. In July, I stood shoulder to shoulder with Navajo Tribal Chairman Peter MacDonald outside of the Four Seasons Hotel in Albuquerque as we addressed the caravan participants. In 1975, I began working with Miriam Crawford and the Navajo-Hopi Unity Committee as we campaigned for the repeal of the so-called Navajo-Hopi Land Settlement Act.

In 1977, I began working with the Big Mountain Committee Against Fencing (which later became the Big Mountain Diné Nation). A year later, I worked with Shirley Martin and the Navajo Longest Walk Steering Committee, which organized a delegation of youth and elders from Big Mountain, Aneth, and other traditional Navajo communities to go on The Longest Walk to Washington, DC. In 1979, a delegation of youth and elders from Big Mountain walked to the First Mount Taylor Gathering to protest uranium mining on our Turquoise Mountain. The American Indian Environmental Council sponsored the three-day gathering and later helped organize the Fifth International Indian Treaty Council Conference at Big Mountain.

In 1980, international law advocate and interpreter Herb Blatchford and I, as expert witness, accompanied Big Mountain Diné Nation President Roberta Blackgoat and Vice President Kee Shay to the Fourth Bertrand Russell Tribunal on the Rights of the Indians of the Americas in Rotterdam, the Netherlands where we presented group testimony and documentation on major human rights violations resulting from the partition, relocation, and mining on Black Mesa. The tribunal later ruled in favor of our international law case. The historic tribunal ruling represented an important step in our continuing Long Walk for International Justice.

CHAPTER 8

CONTINUING THE LONG WALK
FOR JUSTICE

On New Year's Eve 1978, Carole and I celebrated our first year together. Personally, it was a very good year. Professionally, it was a transitional year for me.

I was no longer with the National Indian Youth Council and its New Mexico Indian Environmental Education Project. Now, I was working as a part-time consultant for the Gallup Indian Community Center, developing a fundraising strategy for the construction of a new Indian Center in Gallup. Reaganomics (budgetary genocide) would later kill our efforts in direct violation of the Navajo-Hopi Rehabilitation Act.

I was also a part-time consultant for the UNM Native American Studies Center and its Institute for Native American Development. Among other things, I researched and wrote a paper on the costs of uranium mining on the Navajo reservation. I titled the paper "Uranium Genocide Sacrifice-Part II." It was, in part, a continuation of Herb Blatchford's classic 1978 essay "Uranium Genocide Sacrifice." I also had paid speaking engagements scheduled from January to May 1979.

Carole was still with NIYC but would be leaving in June to return to Nevada and direct a statewide Indian investigative journalism training project. It was funded by the CETA program of the

Inter-Tribal Council of Nevada (ITCN) in Reno. Native Nevadans for Political Education and Action coordinator Dagmar Thorpe Shaw (Sac and Fox) was working to bring her back to direct the new project, which would be part of Dagmar's program at the ITCN's headquarters. The idea for the project came about after ITCN executive director Harold Wyatt (Washo) invited Carole to be the featured speaker on the national anti-Indian backlash movement at ITCN's Thirteenth Annual Convention in Reno. She also conducted workshops on the backlash movement. That December, a month after her speech and workshops, the new job offer looked solid.

After my scheduled speaking gig at the Newberry Library D'Arcy McNickle Center for the History of the American Indian in Chicago in May, we would get my old war pony Bessie tuned up and lubed, and then Carole and I would hit the road to Reno on June 6, 1979.

———

Former NIYC employees Diana Ortiz (Acoma Pueblo) and Geneva Thompson and former NIYC board director Herb Blatchford had recently formed the American Indian Environmental Council (AIEC). Although I had helped the new organization incorporate, I wasn't really involved in the group's formation the way they were. I spoke at their first official meeting in early December, and it was clear that they needed leadership and direction. However, I was pretty busy with my project consultant work and other matters, so I wasn't in a position to offer them immediate help. A week later, Diana and Geneva came to see me and they wanted help bad. I told them I could help AIEC after my consultant work with the Environmental Education Project and other matters were over. After my consultant work was finished, I met with Winona LaDuke first to tell her what I was going to do. She looked at me and said, "Boy, when you do things, you do them in a big way." I then met with Diana to tell her that I would coordinate the First Mount Taylor Gathering, with AIEC as the lead organization.

I had initially proposed the idea of a gathering at Mount Taylor at a caucus of the Natural Guard (a new anti-nuclear group) at the First National No-Nukes Strategy Conference in Louisville, Kentucky in mid-August 1978. This gathering would protest uranium exploration and development on sacred Indian lands in the Grants Mineral Belt, provided that there was an Indigenous NGO as a sponsor. Mount Taylor is at the center of the regional uranium belt. Anyway, I told Winona and Diana in early January 1979 that I was going away for a while after I helped coordinate the Mount Taylor Gathering for the Environmental Council.

At first, there were just a few of us—Diana, Geneva, Herb, me, Ernie Moquino (Santo Domingo Pueblo), Tony JoJola (Isleta Pueblo), and Naomi Becenti (Navajo). We were soon joined by former NIYC employees Mimi Lopez, Robert Tohe, Frank Cerno (Laguna Pueblo), and former NIYC consultant Hazel James (Navajo). Winona was back in school but promised to return a week before the gathering in late April. Lisa and the rest of the Environmental Education staff and consultants supported the gathering as concerned individuals. After we organized locally, we held a major regional meeting in Gallup. At the meeting, we established a regional coordinating council that included representatives from AIEC, Coalition for Navajo Liberation, Diné Bi Professional Association, Navajo Longest Walk Steering Committee, American Indian Movement, International Indian Treaty Council, and Circle Films, as well as individuals such as former NIYC board director Al Henderson, Navajo medicine man Frank Eriacho, and many others. We then began organizing—regionally, nationally, and internationally, as well as multiculturally.

We primarily reached out to uranium-impacted Indian tribes, pueblos, and communities in the Southwest and other Native groups, such as the Navajo Medicinemen Association, Navajo Ranchers Association, Hopi traditionalists, and the Navajo Uranium Radiation Victims Committee. Nationally, we reached out to the Lakota Treaty Council and the Iroquois Confederacy, and internationally to the British Columbia Union of Indian Chiefs, Federation of Saskatchewan Indians, and the Northern Land Council of Australian Aborigines. Our multicultural outreach extended to uranium-affected non-Indian groups and alliances, such as the San Mateo Legal Defense Fund, Sandoval Environmental Action Community, and the Black Hills Alliance.

As AIEC gathering coordinator, it was my responsibility to raise funds for the Indian-led physical and spiritual protest. Fortunately, I was pretty well connected to the funding world. I initially raised money from my old friends and colleagues W.H. Ferry, Carol Bernstein, and Tom Campbell. A fellow member of the Natural Guard Fund, Tom also got me on the new MUSE (Musicians United for Safe Energy) Foundation board (which included a mix of musicians and activists, such as Jackson Browne, Bonnie Raitt, John Hall, Graham Nash, Sam Lovejoy, Harvey Wasserman, Howard Kohn, Tom Hayden, and other quality folks) that raised more money for the gathering and beyond. The national MUSE Foundation board also gave me a certain status among progressive movement funders. I was able to meet personally with Drummond Pike and Marty Tiedel (of the Youth Project, the Shalan Foundation, and the Tides Foundation), who both came to Albuquerque on a site visit that spring. Dan Bomberry (Cayuga-Salish) of the Tribal Sovereignty Program was also interested in funding us with a large donor-advised grant from the Rockefeller Brothers Fund. It took a while to get it, but when we did, the grant had a tremendous impact on the effectiveness of our work.

———

After The Longest Walk, Shirley Martin worked with the Diné Bi Professional Association on the Navajo relocation issue. She then worked as a consultant with the New Mexico Indian Environmental Education Project and, at the time of her death in the spring of 1979, was organizing support for the Mount Taylor Gathering. She was a senior at the University of California at Berkeley and had served as our liaison with the broad-based Bay Area Coalition Against Uranium Mining. She was scheduled to graduate in May. Her classmates asked me to speak in her honor during Native American Week at UC Berkeley. I, of course, said that I would, and did. Shirley Martin was a remarkable organizer and moved mountains in her short lifetime. Taken away far too soon, our dear sister had now joined Larry Casuse, Fred Johnson, Don Noble, and Elva Benson in the spirit world.

———

Although I was no longer with NIYC, I continued to serve on the New Mexico State Advisory Committee (SAC) to the US Civil Rights Commission. At SAC meetings in Santa Fe and Grants in March and April of 1979, we agreed that Grants was an extremely racist bordertown and hostile energy boomtown that needed to be put on the national map like we put Gallup and Farmington on the map in 1973 and 1974. At the Grants meeting, we met with John Dulles II and began planning to conduct a major federal civil rights investigation followed by significant public hearings and a substantial report with solid recommendations. The plan was to hit Grants—the Uranium Capital of the World—where they lived. Stomp their radioactive guts out.

I also continued to serve on the National Council of Churches (NCC) Energy Study Panel, which was finalizing an important policy statement on the ethical implications of energy production and use in America. Northern Cheyenne tribal judge Marie Sanchez and I had jointly presented a strong Native American perspective at a historic conference of the NCC energy study panel in Stony Point, New York in 1977. We were confident that our powerful presentation would be reflected in the final wording of the influential policy document. I was also investigating how to procure ample church funding based on the moral force and universal reach of the document.

On March 12, 1979, Carole left the NIYC building and immediately joined the rest of us at our new gathering headquarters in Old Town. For the next six weeks, we organized with greater efficiency—thanks to Carole's diverse and enhanced professional skill

set. Suffice to say, the gathering was a huge success. The mass pop-
ular uranium resistance movement was just getting started. In the
enduring words of fellow gathering organizer Winona LaDuke:

> The weekend of April 27–29, 1979 marked a turning point
> in Indian resistance, and may even herald the beginning
> of the end of the source of the nuclear fuel cycle. On those
> days, thousands of Navajo and Pueblo Indians—joined by
> Chicano and Anglo supporters—physically and spiritually
> protested uranium mining on Native lands. The demon-
> strations occurred at Mount Taylor, New Mexico, a sacred
> mountain to local Natives and the site of a Gulf Oil-owned
> underground uranium mine—the deepest of its kind in the
> world. Beyond the implications of bringing one hundred
> million pounds of uranium from deep within the earth to
> the surface, the people view this mine as an act of sacrilege
> and desecration.

After the gathering, Carole and I finalized our plans to go to Nevada.
She had a job waiting for her. I had a possible job waiting for me. I
would formally apply for it once we got up there in early June.

In May, I met with Pauline Sice of the Gallup Indian Community
Center and Roxanne Dunbar-Ortiz of the UNM Native American
Studies Center to inform them of my decision to move. I then met
with Winona LaDuke, Lisa Chavez of the New Mexico Indian
Environmental Education Project, and members of the American
Indian Environmental Council and the newly formed Mount Taylor
Alliance (MTA) to inform them of the same. I then resigned from
the MUSE Foundation board and the New Mexico State Advisory
Committee to the Civil Rights Commission, with the recommendation that they replace me with Diana Ortiz. The MUSE Foundation
board did, but the SAC didn't. This was unfortunate since Diana
would have been the only SAC member from civil rights-challenged
northwestern New Mexico—the subject area of the committee's
current investigation. My appointment to the National Council of
Churches Energy Study Panel would officially end with the issu-

ance of the final energy policy statement. So, a replacement was not necessary.

———

On June 6, Carole, me, and Bessie got on the road to Reno. For the next twenty-four hours and a thousand miles, we followed the signs to Harold's Club to the heart of the Biggest Little City.

After washing up and watering our pony at a nearby gas station, we strolled downtown to the legendary Cal-Neva Casino on Second Street, where we each had the Gambler's Special (endless cups of hot strong black coffee and a generous two-dollar steak and eggs breakfast). Refreshed, we motored up Second Street, past the Reno-Sparks Indian Colony, and then turned south on Rock Boulevard to the joint headquarters of the Inter-Tribal Council of Nevada and the Native Nevadans for Political Education and Action. At eight o'clock on the morning of June 7, we were at 650 South Rock Boulevard, Building 11.

Carole hit the ground running on her job. In terms of my possible job, I tripped and landed on my knees. Although I had plenty of real-life work experience, I didn't have the paper academic credentials for the possible job position, so I just withdrew my application so the other guy could get it. It was their loss. Carole got me on her project instead. The CETA program director said that I was overqualified for the training position, but she cut me some slack. So, more of a trainer than a trainee, I developed curriculum, lectured, wrote research papers, went out for hamburgers, and otherwise helped with Carole's project.

Then, in late July, Bessie and I went back to New Mexico to wrap up one last major loose end—a personal matter. I also visited my son Kayah at his mother's house in Albuquerque. I took them to breakfast at Garcia's Kitchen on Fourth Street.

After that, I met with Diana Ortiz, Lisa Chavez, and Herb Blatchford and generally got caught up on things related to their continuing work. Diana and Herb were still with the American

Indian Environmental Council, but Lisa was no longer with the Environmental Education project (which was not renewed by its organizational sponsor). Lisa, former Environmental Education consultant Jennifer Skeet (Navajo), and former NIYC employee Winona LaDuke had since formed a new group called Southwest Affiliated Organizers (SAO). Out of school for the summer, Winona was working with both SAO in the Southwest and the Black Hills Alliance in Rapid City, South Dakota, which had just held its first Black Hills Gathering.

Everyone in the Four Corners of the Southwest—AIEC, Southwest Affiliated Organizers, and the Mount Taylor Alliance— were working together on the upcoming Florencia Gathering to protest the planned Waste Isolation Pilot Project or Plant (a proposed national military nuclear waste storage site) near Carlsbad. In fact, the organizing headquarters for the Indian Environmental Council, SAO, and Mount Taylor Alliance were situated in the Environmental Education Project's old four-office location in the cavernous Sunbell building on West Central.

There were a few more changes, too. Former NIYC employee Louise Four Horns was now organizing her community, Cañoncito, at the far eastern edge of the Grants Uranium Belt. Another former NIYC employee, Tonia Garcia, returned to Lapwai on the Nez Perce reservation in Idaho. She was also the first Indian woman to pass the Idaho bar examination. As an attorney, Tonia was working in the Indian Law Unit of Idaho Legal Aid Services in Boise and continued to support AIEC and its work. Former NIYC attorney George Harrison moved his private practice from Albuquerque to Farmington, where he established a new law office. He then hired former NIYC employee Esther Keeswood to work with him as a Navajo tribal court advocate and interpreter. Finally, former NIYC employee Arlene Luther moved to Window Rock to begin her nearly thirty-year career with the Navajo Tribal Environmental Protection Agency, which was then headed by my good friend from Farmington, the chemist Harold Tso. After my meeting with

Diana and the others in Albuquerque, I went to Farmington to visit my parents.

While in Farmington, I picked up my mail that included a copy of the final energy policy statement adopted by the National Council of Churches governing board. It was a license to go forthwith to the God House at 475 Riverside Drive in New York City to mobilize financial resources for Natives so that we, as a distinct people of color and elder member of the emerging national majority in the coming paradigm shift, could reach critical mass within the space of enlightened environmental, energy, and social justice. In other words, it was a green light for national church fundraising.

My mail also included three copies of *Wasidu: The Continuing Indian Wars* by Bruce Johansen and Roberto Maestas, with an introduction by John Redhouse. Hot off the press, the 268-page hardback was published by Monthly Review Press in New York and London, England. One copy was for me and the other two copies were for Esther Keeswood and Emma Yazzie. The book had already received favorable reviews from Standing Rock Sioux author Vine Deloria, Jr., AIM executive director Vernon Bellecourt, Survival of American Indians Association national director Hank Adams, and Marlon Brando. Mimi Lopez said that Bruce and Roberto had come to Albuquerque to see me in late June, but I had already moved to Nevada, so they mailed the copies of the book to my parents' address in Farmington.

After I got back to Nevada, Geneva Thompson called and asked me if I could return to New Mexico to help them again. I told her, I don't think so. I'm pretty busy up here. And I was.

———

In mid-August, Carole and I decided to leave our comfortable CETA jobs so that we could have full autonomy to properly address the proposed MX Nuclear Missile System, Sagebrush Rebellion movement, and enlarged energy and water development plans in Nevada and Utah. We co-founded the Nevada Indian Environmental Research

Project and raised funds from W.H. "Ping" Ferry and the Tribal Sovereignty Program to support our high-impact work. For the next four months, we worked directly with the Western Shoshone Sacred Lands Association, United Paiutes, Native Nevadans for Political Education and Action, Inter-Tribal Council of Nevada, and the Paiute Tribe of Utah. By the end of the year (and the decade), there was a sense of intertribal unity that could be built on and strengthened by others to ensure common survival amidst challenges facing the Great Basin—from the Sierra Nevadas to the Wasatch and from the Virgin River to the Snake River.

Early one morning in early January 1980, I awoke and clearly remembered the dream that woke me—a warm wind was blowing strong from the south and tugged at my spirit. I knew I had to go home. I had to go home now.

Later that morning, ITCN receptionist Marilyn Melendez (Pyramid Lake Paiute) called and told me to come to the office at once to sign for a registered parcel sent from Amsterdam, the Netherlands. I rushed right over. The parcel contained a letter and enclosures from Dick de Soeten, a general board member of the Workgroup Indian Project that was working on an International Tribunal. The letter read in part:

> We came in the receipt of your address during the visit at our country by Winona LaDuke and Herbert Blatchford in October 1979. These people told us you could be the right person to coordinate a case for the Tribunal.
>
> The enclosures will tell you about the Tribunal and the way you can prepare the case. It has to be said that if you would prepare and coordinate the Navajo case, we need your papers in Amsterdam before 30 April 1980. It is necessary to also make a written summary of your case in the form of a kind of statement, which can be used as your spoken introduction to the jury and also as a basic document for the press. To give you an idea of such a document, I'll enclose the first page of the Hopi case as it will be spoken in front of the jury. Separate

to the mentioned summary have to belong the necessary documents and/or reports as background information.

Furthermore, we can't give the guarantee that your case will be brought in front of the jury, however we can promise your case, together with a couple more, will appear within a book or document to the notice of the governments concerned, the General Assembly of the United Nations, and general public, including all kind of the governmental and political entities all over the world.

This will be all this time. If you are willing to prepare the Navajo-case, we'd be glad to hear from you soon. If there are any questions, we'd be glad to try to answer them. We do hope to hearing from you soon.

Winona and Herb had gone on a continental speaking tour in Europe in the fall of 1979. When they spoke in the Netherlands, they met with Mr. de Soeten and other members of the Workgroup Indian Project and the Bertrand Russell Peace Foundation, who were organizing the Fourth Russell Tribunal on the Rights of the Indians of the Americas in Rotterdam in November 1980.

———

I raised funds from Ping Ferry to finance our move to Flagstaff, where Carole and I co-founded the Northern Arizona Indian Environmental Research Project and worked with Herb and the Big Mountain Diné Nation to prepare the recently selected Navajo relocation case from January to May. From June to August, I researched and analyzed the political geography of the Black Mesa coal and water basin underlying Big Mountain. I also investigated the geology and hydrology of the uranium-rich Grand Canyon and Colorado Plateau regions of Arizona and Utah. With additional funding from the Tribal Sovereignty Program, we worked with the Western Shoshone Sacred Lands Association in Nevada, which was also selected to present its land rights case at the Tribunal.

In September, Carole and I returned to Albuquerque, where I worked for five months as executive director of the American Indian Environmental Council and facilitator of the Mount Taylor Alliance. Carole immediately found work with the Prime Times Publishing Company as a typographer, graphic artist, and writer for *Prime Times*, a weekly alternative newspaper.

Coincidently, the publishing company and its newspaper were located in the old Sunbell building on West Central and, in fact, occupied most of the same multi-office floor space used by the late New Mexico Indian Environmental Education Project and later by AIEC, Southwest Affiliated Organizers, and the Mount Taylor Alliance before they too left the building in 1979–80. The American Indian Environmental Council and the Mount Taylor Alliance were now headquartered on the second floor of a historic building on East Central in the eclectic Nob Hill District.

After the Dalton Pass Gathering near Crownpoint in April, AIEC and MTA intensified their campaign to protect sacred Indian lands in the Grants Mineral Belt. On the sacredness of the groups' continued work, Herb put it best when he said, "There was a call from Mount Taylor. It was a clear, true call for the people to face a common adversary. Mount Taylor is sacred to the Navajo and the Pueblo. It is one of the mountains created from the sands of the Underworld."

The regional uranium boom was permanently busted and in sharp decline by the end of the year due to their effective campaign and other factors, including the fallout over the recent Three Mile Island and Church Rock radioactive disasters.

When presenting the Navajo relocation case in Rotterdam in November, Herb served as an international legal advocate and interpreter and I was an expert witness. I also served as an expert witness for the Western Shoshone treaty rights case at the Tribunal. Western Shoshone Sacred Lands Association spokeswoman Pearl Dann and I presented the international law case. I even helped the Hotevilla Hopi delegation with additional research and documenta- tion for their case at the Tribunal (as it related to ordered Hopi relocation from federally partitioned, energy-rich lands by the federal Navajo and Hopi Indian Relocation Commission under the 1974 Navajo-Hopi Land Settlement Act).

The Tribunal and other international fora soon led to the establishment of the United Nations Working Group on Indigenous Populations, which later drafted the UN Declaration on the Rights of Indigenous Peoples.

———

In late January 1981, I resigned as executive director of the American Indian Environmental Council and facilitator of the Mount Taylor Alliance. I was a little burned out from the past nine years. I was planning to go back to school in June. In the meantime, I was going to spend more time with my son, go on some road trips with my parents, have a beer with my brother, and see my sister and her family.

ABOUT THE AUTHOR

John Redhouse was born and raised in Farmington, New Mexico and graduated from Farmington High School in 1969. He was a longtime Navajo and Indian rights activist. Redhouse worked with the Indians Against Exploitation in Gallup, NM in 1972–1973 and the Coalition for Navajo Liberation in Farmington in 1974. He was Associate Director of the National Indian Youth Council in Albuquerque, NM from 1974 to 1978. Redhouse also served on the City of Albuquerque-Bernalillo County Air Quality Control Board in 1978 and the New Mexico State Advisory Committee to the United States Civil Rights Commission in 1978–79. In 1979–1980, he worked with the American Indian Environmental Council in Albuquerque; Reno, Nevada; and Flagstaff, Arizona. Redhouse was a writer and consultant from 1981 to 1987. In 1988–1989, he worked with the Tonantzin Land Institute in Albuquerque. Redhouse was a consultant from 1990 to 2012. He is a graduate of the University of New Mexico and a U.S. Army veteran.

ABOUT THE CONTRIBUTORS

Jennifer Denetdale is a citizen of the Navajo Nation. She is a professor of American Studies at the University of New Mexico and the chair of the Navajo Nation Human Rights Commission. She is the author of *Reclaiming Diné History: The Legacies of Navajo Chief Manuelito and Juanita* and two Diné histories for young adults. She is a co-author of *Red Nation Rising: From Bordertown Violence to Native Liberation* and has published numerous journal articles and chapter essays on Indigenous feminisms, Diné nation building, and bordertown studies. She is the recipient of two Henry Luce Foundation grants to mount a Milton Snow Photography exhibition in collaboration with the Navajo Nation Museum.

Melanie K. Yazzie (Diné) is an assistant professor of American Indian Studies at the University of Minnesota-Twin Cities and co-author of *Red Nation Rising: From Bordertown Violence to Native Liberation* and *The Red Deal: Indigenous Action to Save the Earth.* She co-hosts and produces the podcast Red Power Hour, which is sponsored by Red Media, a Native-led media organization she co-founded in 2019. She also does community organizing with The Red Nation, a grassroots Native-run organization she co-founded in 2014 that is committed to Indigenous liberation and decolonization.

ABOUT COMMON NOTIONS

Common Notions is a publishing house and programming platform that fosters new formulations of living autonomy. We aim to circulate timely reflections, clear critiques, and inspiring strategies that amplify movements for social justice.

Our publications trace a constellation of critical and visionary meditations on the organization of freedom. By any media necessary, we seek to nourish the imagination and generalize common notions about the creation of other worlds beyond state and capital. Inspired by various traditions of autonomism and liberation—in the US and internationally, historical and emerging from contemporary movements—our publications provide resources for a collective reading of struggles past, present, and to come.

Common Notions regularly collaborates with political collectives, militant authors, radical presses, and maverick designers around the world. Our political and aesthetic pursuits are dreamed and realized with Antumbra Designs.

www.commonnotions.org
info@commonnotions.org

BECOME A COMMON NOTIONS MONTHLY SUSTAINER

These are decisive times ripe with challenges and possibility, heart-ache, and beautiful inspiration. More than ever, we need timely reflections, clear critiques, and inspiring strategies that can help movements for social justice grow and transform society.

Help us amplify those words, deeds, and dreams that our liberation movements, and our worlds, so urgently need.

Movements are sustained by people like you, whose fugitive words, deeds, and dreams bend against the world of domination and exploitation.

For collective imagination, dedicated practices of love and study, and organized acts of freedom.
By any media necessary.
With your love and support.

Monthly sustainers start at $15 and receive each new book in our publishing program.

commonnotions.org/sustain